Developing
Executive Skills

Managing Yourself, Others, and Organizations

By John R. Hook

VELOCITY BUSINESS PUBLISHING, INC.
BRISTOL, VERMONT USA

For Pat, who taught us the most important life lessons.

Copyright © 2001 by John R. Hook

All Rights Reserved

Library of Congress Catalog Card Number 2001094089

ISBN 1-58099-033-9

Cover design by Susan Vigsnes

Printed in Canada

If you'd like a catalog of books in the Agile Gold Series™ or the Agile Manager Series®, please get in touch.

- **Write us:**

    Velocity Business Publishing, Inc.

    15 Main Street

    Bristol, VT 05443 USA

- **Call us:**

    1-888-805-8600 in North America (toll-free)

    1-802-453-6669 from all other countries

- **Fax us:**

    1-802-453-2164

- **E-mail us:**

    action@agilemanager.com

- **Visit our Web site:**

    www.agilemanager.com

    The Web site has much of interest to business people, including management tips, online courses, e-books for handhelds, audiotapes, and much more.

♦

Contents

◆

Preface

This is a book for the busy executive or senior manager seeking an edge in performance, and for younger managers seeking skill development and insights on senior-level management. My intent is that it will find its way into a variety of settings: in the briefcase of the manager on a business trip, in vacation beach bags, at bedside and poolside—any place that will lend itself to some quiet reflection.

The content was inspired by my experience consulting with senior managers in business, government, and non-profit organizations over the past twenty years. Much of what is here I learned from them. In the course of conducting hundreds of seminars and workshops, I've watched executives suddenly awaken intellectually to what they already knew instinctively, and I've been impressed by the tremendous growth that takes place in that process. Over the years people would often approach me after a workshop, tell me how much they had gained from the experience, and ask if the material existed in written form. Unfortunately, the answer was always no. I never seemed to have the time to publish it. But the notion of a book, to make the material available to a wider audience, finally became compelling.

This book is organized into three parts: Managing Yourself, Managing Others, and Managing Organizations. Each part has six modules on such topics as Enhancing Creativity, Managing Change, and Organization Assessment. Each module has five sections:

Typical Situation: A short, fictional anecdote describing a manager with a problem relating to the topic.

Central Ideas: A concise discussion of the important concepts; just enough theory to guide action.

Situation Revisited: A continuation of the typical situation. The manager uses the concepts to solve the problem or improve the situation.

Application: Questions, exercises, and suggested actions to personalize the concepts and apply them to your personal and organizational situation.

Bottom Lines: Several major points about the topic; summary points.

Each module is designed to stand alone. While I encourage you to progress through all the modules, they can be undertaken in any order that meets your interests or needs. The material has been designed to be easy to read.

The theory (*Central Ideas*) is clearly and concisely stated, with the busy reader in mind. Some of the information is anecdotal because it is my conviction that the best approach to learning management is experiential. We learn what works by trying things ourselves and by watching others experiment in the workplace. I relate my own observations and experiences to encourage you to dig deeply into your own well of experience, where I am confident you will find many of your own answers, answers most valid for you and your work.

Acknowledgments

Many people contributed to this book. Some shared their most creative ideas, others their technical skills, and many their encouragement and support. I am indebted to them all and it is with pleasure that I mention a few by name:

—Professors Frank Sherwood, Bob Biller, and the late Neely Gardner of the University of Southern California. Neely shared his tested techniques on consulting and organization assessment, Bob his unique concepts on planning and change, and Frank— let's just say he taught me most of what I know about organization theory and adult learning.

—Professors Monty Kast and Jim Rosenzweig of the University of Washington, who first introduced me to the notion of systems thinking and graciously allowed me to use their systems model in this book.

—Professor Charlie Beitz, my colleague at both the Army War College and Mount Saint Mary's College. Charlie and I have been friends for many years and collaborators on numerous projects; he is a deep and creative thinker and I confess to stealing many of his ideas.

—Jeff Olson, my editor at Velocity Business Publishing, a past master at drawing out the best from you through his gentle guidance. Jeff's eye for detail and ability to sharpen a phrase has significantly improved the quality of this book. And he's so easy to work with—we solved dozens of problems with one-minute telephone conversations or three lines of e-mail.

—Becky Brown, secretary for the Business Department at Mount Saint Mary's College, and the only human being who can read my handwriting. Becky's enthusiasm spurred me on as she compensated for my lack of technical skill by typing the various drafts. Though she supports sixteen faculty members, she was always ready to move my work to the top of the pile.

—My children: Mark, Carol, and Cathy, and their spouses— my thanks for their continuing interest, encouragement, and support. Special thanks to Carol, my "first editor" on any writing project. Carol has an uncanny ability to improve my writing while still honoring the idiosyncrasies of my style. She was a full collaborator on this book, contributing to both the writing quality and the content in a major way.

—Finally, I must mention my wife, Pat. Always a one-person cheering section for each member of our family, she remains with us in spirit, inspiring us to do our best. As I wrote this book, I found myself imagining her comments—and that has made it a better book. This book is dedicated to you Pat—God Bless!

♦

Introduction

This book is structured around the three major skill areas required of managers: managing yourself, managing others, and managing organizations.

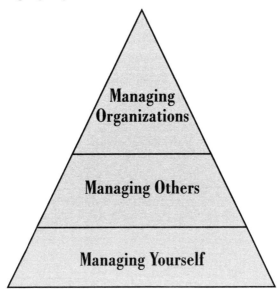

The diagram says it all. Managing yourself is a necessary foundation. We cannot manage others without first mastering the skills of self-management. And, since management involves getting things done through others, we need sound skills in managing others before attempting to manage the entire organization. The whole here is clearly greater than the sum of the parts.

The book addresses eighteen skill topics—six in each of the three major skill areas. The topics were selected largely on the basis of my personal experience conducting seminars for senior managers. I selected the topics managers say they most need. I also reviewed the course content of the executive management programs of twelve major universities as a check on my own instincts. The result is the following organization of the book.

Managing Yourself
—Conceptual Thinking: *Using Theory to Guide Action*
—Enhancing Style Range: *Adding Tools to Your Kit Bag*
—Enhancing Creativity: *Thinking the Unthinkable*
—Time Management: *Spending Time Where It's Needed*
—Stress Management: *Rolling with the Punch*
—Life and Career Planning: *Deciding What You Want— and How to Get It*

Managing Others
—Motivation: *Getting People Moving—in Right Directions*
—Leadership: *Setting the Course—and Inspiring Followership*
—Negotiation, Influence, and Power: *Picking the Lock vs. Breaking Down the Door*
—Managing Interpersonal Relations and Conflict:

Capitalizing on Differences
—Managing Groups: *Building Teamwork*
—Human Resources Management: *Checking the System*

Managing Organizations
—A Systems Approach to Management: *Seeing the Parts—and the Whole*
—Analysis of the External Environment: *Tackling the Outside World*
—Organizational Culture: *Answering—What Are We Like; How Should We Be?*
—Organization Assessment: *Finding What's Going Right—and Wrong*
—Planning: *Preparing for the Future*
—Managing Change: *Making It Easy—Getting It Done*

In deciding what to say and how much to say on each topic, I leaned heavily on my seminar experiences. It always seemed to me that experienced managers already knew a lot about each of these topics. Down deep they knew the answers to their critical problems. What they typically lacked was the time and inclination to be reflective about their performance, to ask themselves the right questions.

That's where I feel my particular seminar approach was most helpful. It started by identifying some central conceptual ideas about the topics. Then it caused the participants to be reflective in assessing personal styles, strengths, and weaknesses. Finally, it turned their attention to possible actions for individual and organizational improvement.

That approach worked well in the seminars, and I've tried to use the same approach to this book. It provides the full array of topics deserving attention.

Under each topic there is a section titled *Typical Situation* which provides a short, fictional anecdote describing a manager with a problem relating to the topic. This is followed by a more extensive section titled *Central Ideas,* which provides a conceptual framework for thinking about the topic. Next you'll find the *Situation Revisited* where the manager reflects on the concepts and uses them to solve the problem or improve the typical situation. This is followed by a section titled *Application,* which has questions, exercises, and suggested actions to help you make the concepts your own. Finally, there is a short section called *Bottom Lines* to capture a few of the most important points.

To sum up, the material here closely follows what has proven effective in the seminars. The book may actually be the more effective approach. It is certainly more time efficient than attending seminars. But, beyond that, having the full array of topics available allows you to focus time in the areas of greatest need.

Part One

Managing Yourself

- ◆ MODULE ONE: **Conceptual Thinking**
  Using Theory to Guide Action

- ◆ MODULE TWO: **Enhancing Style Range**
  Adding Tools to Your Kit Bag

- ◆ MODULE THREE: **Enhancing Creativity**
  Thinking the Unthinkable

- ◆ MODULE FOUR: **Time Management**
  Spending Time Where It's Needed

- ◆ MODULE FIVE: **Stress Management**
  Rolling with the Punch

- ◆ MODULE SIX: **Life and Career Planning**
  Deciding What You Want—and How to Get It

Conceptual Thinking:
Using Theory to Guide Action

Typical Situation

Matt Archer, newly promoted to vice president of research for a large multinational computer software firm, stared at the big stack of books on his desk. The firm was sending him to the Advanced Management Program at UCLA, a six-week intensive program taught several times annually to groups of executives on the way to the top. This was homework, to be completed before attending the program. His executive assistant, Kathy Wolfe (a recent graduate from a local executive MBA program), came in.

"What's all that?"

"My homework for UCLA."

"Looks like a lot of work."

"That's what I think. Looks like a lot of useless theory."

"No, it'll be useful; you'll see."

"How so?"

"It will make it easier to think through tough problems. Theory always helps. You use it now, you just don't think about it. The great thing about a bit of course work now and then is that it makes us conscious of theory we already know from experience, plus it gives us some new ideas. And most important, it encourages us to use our theory to see into situations more clearly and make better decisions."

"You sound convinced."

"I am. Had a professor who called it conceptual thinking—using theory to guide action. I've become a believer."

"OK, I'll give it try."

Central Ideas

Conceptual thinking can be described as using theory to guide action. It implies being deliberate and reflective. It is the opposite of "winging it."

How much theory must you know to qualify as a conceptual thinker? Actually, less theory than you probably already know, even if you have had little formal management training. Theory isn't something that you get primarily from books. Books can help—I hope this one does. But theory is your personal truth about what works for you in managerial situations. That truth, that theory, is largely obtained from experience—your own personal observations of approaches that have worked (or failed to work) for you and for others. Every experienced manager has a lot of such truths.

Let me illustrate with an example of an exercise that I've used hundreds of times in management seminars. Participants are put in small groups of five or six and given ten minutes to reach a decision regarding the following situation:

> Assume you are in a decision-making group in the trauma center of a large metropolitan hospital. It is late at night. Four injured people have been simultaneously

brought into the trauma center, the victims of a vehicle accident. The four injured people are: a sixteen-year-old girl, a thirty-year-old priest, a thirty-five-year-old widow with six small children, and a fifty-year-old, well-known medical doctor reportedly near a critical breakthrough in developing an AIDS immunization. The victims all need the same piece of life-support equipment, the center has only one piece of that equipment, and the trauma center doctors say the person given the equipment will very likely fully recover and live a normal life span. The other three can be expected to die in less than an hour. The group is told it must decide within ten minutes whom to put on that equipment.

You can imagine the kind of discussion that follows. To conclude the exercise I ask participants to focus on two areas of theory: values and assumptions. We use the group experience to develop individual "truths" (i.e., theory) about values and assumptions.

Participants have just observed others make various statements reflecting values: "we need to give that young girl a chance at life"; "that family has to be held together"; "that doctor can save thousands of lives"; "that priest can save thousands of souls."

They have also heard statements reflecting assumptions: "Some other family member will care for those children"; "the doctor would have his work documented"; "the priest would sacrifice his life for others." After this discussion, two statements of theory become obvious to participants:

◆ **KEY QUOTE** ◆

"Thinking is the hardest work there is, which is the probable reason so few engage in it."
—Henry Ford

● Values of individuals differ and affect their decisions.
● Assumptions of individuals differ and affect their decisions.

All participants believe these two theories at the conclusion of the exercise because they have just experienced the
theories in action. At this point you are probably saying to
yourself that you knew these theories all along, that you have
seen value and assumption differences played out in many
group decision-making settings. I'm sure you have. Actually, it makes my point: We all carry around a lot of truths or
theories from our experiences.

The trick is to recognize the theories we know and to use
those theories. Theory isn't just something to know, it is something to help us act. Theory is useful in two ways:

● As a lens to see with.
● As a guide to designing managerial actions.

Both uses are examples of conceptual thinking: using
theory to guide action.

Let's look at an example to illustrate. Suppose one of my
personal theories includes the statement that individuals'
values differ and impact their decisions. Suppose further that
I am confronted with an organizational problem. Assume I'm
an entrepreneur, in retailing. I started my business thirty
years ago, and at that point I was the only employee. I did
the buying, operated the store, delivered purchases, repaired
TVs, kept the books. Now I have ten stores and a fairly large
organization.

Assume further that until now I've always been in a growth
situation, but financial difficulties demand that I now downsize. Specifically, I must lay off four of my twelve buyers.

Suppose I elect to downsize by appointing a selection board to review the records of the twelve buyers and name the four to let go. Suppose further that I want to enhance the probability of a particular outcome—I want to be sure that all considerations (e.g., seniority, efficiency, financial need) get a fair hearing.

Who would I put on the board? Well, if I use my theory (and I should), I'd want a group with diverse values. I'd probably select some senior people (who would value seniority), some young hard chargers (who would value efficiency), and someone who would likely be sensitive to the financial need issue.

This example illustrates a manager in the act of conceptual thinking: using his theory (values differ and affect decisions) to design his managerial action (picking the members of the selection board).

Situation Revisited

Fast forward six weeks. Matt returns to work and Kathy spots him.

"How was UCLA, Matt?"

"Great."

"Learn a lot of theory?"

"Yeah, a good bit. But the most important thing I have learned is to think conceptually by using my theory."

"They push that?"

"Nope, never mentioned it. I got that idea from you, and I'm very grateful. It will change the way I do things."

"How so?"

"Well, we worked on cases in teams at UCLA and one thing that really impressed me—and sort of surprised me too—was what different assumptions we all made as we analyzed the cases. That's a piece of theory I intend to use to help our task force that's studying the air force contract."

"How does that apply?"

"Well, their task is to make a recommendation on which of two prototypes we continue working on. One has to be abandoned at this point. I realize they are going to have to make assumptions about a lot of things: technical capabilities, user friendliness, production costs, required maintenance services. I want to avoid bad or unnecessary assumptions that will waste their time or result in a recommendation we can't support. So I plan to do a number of things: Get them fully briefed at the start, meet with them frequently to review their assumptions, and make sure everyone in the organization recognizes the need to respond quickly to their requests for information. In short, I'm going to follow all assumptions carefully—just like my theory says."

> ◆ **KEY QUOTE** ◆
>
> **"People don't seem to realize that it takes time and effort and preparation to think."**
> **—Bertrand Russell**

Kathy returned to her office and thought, "Smart guy. I guess I did help a little. But he really picked up on that idea of conceptual thinking. We are going to be a good team."

Application

❑ Do you make it a practice to scan your managerial experiences and observations to generalize theories (truths) that can guide your future actions? If not, start by drawing conclusions from your daily experiences.

◆   ◆   ◆

❑ State one of your favorite theories and how you developed it. For example, one of mine is: When you assume a new managerial position, respect the existing culture. I learned that from watching a boss alienate an organization by disregarding the culture.

◆   ◆   ◆

❑ When assessing a managerial situation or making a managerial decision, are you normally conscious of being guided by the theories (truths) generated by your experiences?

◆   ◆   ◆

❑ State an instance when your theory guided your action. (If you're having trouble, think back to an important decision you made recently. It's likely values or assumptions played a part in it.)

◆   ◆   ◆

❑ Two of my theories are:
—People balk at abrupt changes made by new leaders.
—People improve most effectively when they receive frequent, timely, off-the-record verbal feedback on performance.
State one of your own personal theories or use one of mine. Then describe a situation where it was or could have been used to guide action.

◆   ◆   ◆

❑ Make a list of your five most valued theories. Resolve to make the effort to keep building your list of theories, and to use them to guide your actions.

Bottom Lines

➤ Your theory is your truth about what works for you in managerial situations.

➤ Theory can be suggested by books, but ultimately it must be tested or validated through experience to be truly believed. Sometimes theory comes solely from experience.

➤ Theory is useful as a lens to see with and as a guide to action. Using it in either way is called conceptual thinking: a very deliberate and systematic approach to solving problems.

◆ Module Two ◆

Enhancing Style Range:
Adding Tools to Your Kit Bag

Typical Situation

Ann Wilson, one of twenty plant managers of a large candy manufacturing company, has a big problem. It is noon on Halloween and one of her distributors just notified her that a customer had called to report that a piece of the firm's candy was thought to be contaminated (it had made the family dog instantly sick).

Ann suddenly feels ill herself. She could be in big trouble. This is a very bottom-line firm, expecting huge sales from all its plants on this particular day. Ann's a plant manager for one big reason: She focuses on that bottom line, always delivers. She's got to deliver today, and will. "But," she thinks, "better get the team together, talk it over, get a consensus. It's probably nothing, but it needs to be discussed."

Central Ideas

We all have a preference for certain styles in dealing with

management issues. For example:

- As leaders, we may prefer a collaborative to an auto-cratic approach.
- In negotiating, we may prefer a hard to a soft approach.
- In conflict situations, we may prefer to compete rather than to compromise.
- We may prefer to base decisions primarily on bottom line facts rather than peoples' feelings or matters of social responsibility.

It is entirely appropriate to have style preferences. It would be impossible to avoid. However, different circumstances require different styles. Thus, full effectiveness means enhancing your style range, to equip yourself with the necessary styles to meet any challenge.

Initially, it might seem difficult to expand your style range. But actually it's quite easy. It is simply a matter of recognizing your preferred style as just one style among a number of others, and then forcing yourself to consider the use of the other styles in appropriate situations.

In later sections of this book I'll be suggesting you expand your style range in a variety of management-skill areas (e.g., leadership, conflict management, influence). But to capture the basic notion of style-range enhancement, let's look now at the relationship between individual personality and the things that typically concern managers in making organizational decisions.

To do this, let's first make a rough assessment of your personality. A widely used evaluation instrument in management development is the Myers-Briggs personality instrument. If the idea of getting a fully accurate measure of your personality type intrigues you, any management trainer could arrange for you to be tested. But for our purposes here, a very simple measure should be sufficient.

The Myers-Briggs instrument gives a four letter designator for personality. The first letter tells you if you are an extroverted (E) or introverted (I) person; the second letter if you are sensing (S) or intuitive (N); the third letter if you are thinking (T) or feeling (F); and the fourth letter if you are judging (J) or perceiving (P).

Using the simple definitions below, try making a crude assessment of your personality type. To do this pick the one letter from each pair that you think best fits you. Circle your four letters below.

E for <u>extroversion</u> means you probably relate more easily to the outer world of people and things than to the inner world of ideas.	**I** for <u>introversion</u> means you probably relate more easily to the inner world of ideas than to the outer world of people and things.
S for <u>sensing</u> means you probably would rather work with known facts than look for possibilities and relationships.	**N** for <u>intuitive</u> means you probably would rather look for possibilities and relationships than work with known facts.
T for <u>thinking</u> means you probably base your judgements more on impersonal analysis and logic than on personal values.	**F** for <u>feeling</u> means you probably base your judgments more on personal values than on impersonal analysis and logic.
J for <u>judging</u> means you probably like a planned, predictable, orderly way of life better than a flexible, spontaneous way.	**P** for <u>perceiving</u> means you probably like a flexible, spontaneous way of life better than a planned, predictable, orderly way.

Your personality type has implications for the way you like to work and for the issues that concern you the most. For example, dominant organizational concerns of managers tend to vary by personality type, as follows:

ST: worry about bottom line issues, such as units produced per hour, sales per salesperson or employee, sales per marketing dollar spent, net profit, and rate of return on capital.

SF: worry about internal personnel issues, such as interpersonal relationships, employee attitudes and grievances, team effectiveness, and organizational culture and climate.

NF: worry about external concerns, such as social responsibility, customer satisfaction, and community satisfaction with the organization.

NT: worry about such external concerns as cost of labor, cost of capital, cost of raw materials, trade issues, and government regulations.

Stop now, and with your best guess about your personality type in mind, ask yourself the following questions:

- What does my personality type indicate about my primary organizational concerns?
- Would I enhance my effectiveness if I could make myself worry about all of the concerns mentioned above?

I think the answer is obvious. Solving tough organizational problems normally involves dealing with multiple concerns: the financial bottom line, the impact on employees, the attitudes of customers, and the concerns of the community. Effective decision making demands that all such concerns be considered. That means the effective manager must have sufficient style range to take a balanced view of problems.

Tough to do? Not really. The good news is that you can train yourself, actually "will" yourself, to consider all these concerns. All that is necessary is to know your personal inclination (i.e., your personality style) and to deliberately direct your attention to issues in your blind spots. It's easy, actually. And so important!

A few years ago I had the opportunity to act as facilitator of a teambuilding workshop at a large community college. The dean had sensed the need for this session because he was experiencing a great deal of conflict at meetings with two new Assistant Deans. He was beginning to think he'd made bad hiring decisions. At the workshop everyone completed the Myers-Briggs instrument. The dean was an ISTJ and both assistant deans had the opposite style (ENFP). No surprise they clashed so vigorously.

> ◆ **KEY QUOTE** ◆
>
> **"The top management tasks require at least four different kinds of human beings: the person of thought, the person of action, the 'people person' and the 'front man.'"**
> **—Peter F. Drucker**

But real development occurred at this workshop. You could see it happening. Both the dean and his assistant deans recognized three things. First, they saw that their differences in viewpoint were caused by personality differences, not obstinacy; so no need to be angry. Second, they recognized that extending their individual styles would make them more effective as individuals, enable them to better see the big picture. And finally, they left the workshop convinced that this blend of personality styles on the team was a strength, not a weakness. It ensured they would not miss important issues in the decision-making process.

Situation Revisited

Ann's management team assembles and hears her story and conclusion: "It's probably nothing. This is the biggest sales day of the year. I don't think we can let ourselves be distracted by one crazy call, about a sick dog, no less. But I thought we ought to at least get together."

Then it started, a veritable free-for-all. Everyone seemed to shout at once.

"Are you crazy, Ann? This could be very serious."

"The firm's reputation is a lot more important than one day of sales at our plant."

"What if some child should be poisoned?"

"Think about the possible community reaction. Even if the report turns out to be wrong, what would people think of us if we did not act responsibly right now?"

◆ **KEY QUOTE** ◆

"The principle source of erroneous judgement is viewing things partially and only on one side."
—Samuel Johnson

"Let's get the word out now: radio, TV, calls to distributors. Get our candy off the shelves immediately and warn the community. Tonight is Halloween!"

Ann was stunned. "They are right," she thought. "How could I have had such a blind spot, such a fixation on the bottom line? I've got to start taking a better look at the big picture. But right now I've got to work quickly, get that word out!"

Application

❑ Think about some of the difficult decisions your team has faced in the past.

—Who pushed hard for those concerns listed as ST, SF, NF, NT?

—Was the team sufficiently diverse so that all types of concerns got considered?

—Did all the diverse concerns get treated with appropriate respect?

◆　　◆　　◆

❑ With the above examples in mind, try to guess the personality type of each member of your team. Do you feel you have sufficient diversity on the team to get healthy debate and creative solutions to problems?

◆　　◆　　◆

❑ Now think about your own approach to some current complex organizational situation demanding your attention.

—Consider whether your primary concerns in this situation are the concerns listed as ST, SF, NF, or NT.

—Force yourself to think of this situation using the full range of concerns: ST, SF, NF, and NT.

—Note whether expanding your style range to include this full range of concerns provides you with additional insights into the situation or directs you to any new action areas.

◆　　◆　　◆

❑ Resolve, on future problems, to extend your style range, and encourage others to do the same.

◆　　◆　　◆

❑ If you suspect it could help your team be more creative, arrange for the team to take the Myers-Briggs instrument, share their results, and discuss the implications of style differences on the team.

Bottom Lines

➤ We all have style preferences.
➤ Leading diverse groups and dealing with complex situations demands multiple styles.
➤ We must, and we can, expand our range of styles to meet the needs of different subordinates and situations.

◆ Module Three ◆

Enhancing Creativity:
Thinking the Unthinkable

Typical Situation

Ed Ryan, provost of a small liberal arts college, is concerned. For the past five years there has been a gradual decrease in applications for admission to the college. The admissions director is energetic and experienced, and he seems effective in pushing his people to intensify their recruiting efforts. But what worries Ed is the absence of new ideas. Admissions seems to just be pushing harder at the same old approaches. He has just left a meeting with all the admissions staff and heard the same old excuses:

—"The college age population is shrinking in the areas where we recruit."
—"Our staff is limited; we can't cover any more 'College Nights' at high schools than we now do."
—"If you'd only let us hire more staff . . ."

How can he unlock the creativity he senses is there? How can he tap his own creativity to guide them?

Central Ideas

Few things have such payoff in improved performance as time spent on enhancing individual creativity. And there are few things easier to do than to improve one's ability to think more creatively.

Three simple approaches have proven useful to me in helping managers improve creativity:

- Doing creativity exercises.
- Focusing on obstacles to creativity.
- Discovering the power of shifting paradigms to reframe complex problems into a more manageable form.

Let me ask you to first attempt to solve two creativity puzzles or exercises. Don't look at the solutions (on the next page) until you have tried to solve each puzzle.

Dots Exercise

Draw four straight lines through the nine dots below without retracing and without lifting your pen from the paper.

Watch Exercise

A man dropped his watch and the face broke into 4 parts. The numbers on each of the broken pieces add up to 15. Draw a picture of how the watch may have been broken.

Dots Solution. You may have found it easy to solve the dots exercise. But most people find it difficult. The typical approach is to try to solve the puzzle by drawing lines within the box formed by the outer dots. But the puzzle can't be solved by staying within the box. Here's one correct solution:

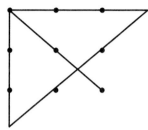

Note that you must "get out of the box" to solve this puzzle. The broader creativity message from this exercise is that we often fail to think creatively because we feel constrained by artificial boundaries. We must think of solutions beyond the boundaries of "our boxes."

Watch Solution. A solution to the watch exercise is shown below.

The key to the solution requires seeing that the numbers on the larger (right hand) piece can be viewed and added as follows: 1+1+1+2+1+2+3+4 = 15. Few people solve this puzzle correctly. Some get a bit annoyed when they see the solution; they feel they've been tricked. But again there is a broader creativity message from the exercise: You must look at problems in unconventional ways if you seek truly creative solutions.

A second approach to enhancing creativity is to look at the mindsets that often pose obstacles to creativity, and to work on removing these obstacles. Five typical mindsets that form obstacles to creativity are:

1. *"There is a 'right' answer."* Sometimes there is one right answer. But many problems have several "approximately right" answers, and these need to be explored. Searching for "the one right answer" can blind you to the full range of possibilities that may exist in any situation.

2. *"I must be logical and follow the rules."* The best way to find a good idea is to generate a lot of ideas for further evaluation. There certainly is a time to be logical, but logic should not be a limiting factor when developing initial ideas on a problem. Also, the rules may become important when evaluating possible solutions, but you should not let existing rules confine you as you develop tentative solutions.

3. *"I must not make a mistake."* The fear of error often inhibits creativity. You must ignore that fear and concerns about being wrong or seeming foolish to truly release your creativity. And, importantly, managers must help subordinates overcome this fear as well. Some manufacturing plants hang signs saying: "This is a zero-defects organization." And some bosses publicly criticize subordinates who suggest "wild ideas." Such practices are powerful blocks to creativity because they make people afraid to offer ideas.

4. "I must not tread on another's turf." The "that's not my area" syndrome is one of the greatest blocks to overall organizational creativity. And this is where good leadership can foster both individual and group creativity. The leader must make people feel free to offer suggestions in matters beyond their own specific areas of responsibility. Organizations cannot be creative if they allow thinking to be bounded by the lines on the organizational chart.

5. "I'm not very creative." We all have the capacity to be creative. But many people fail to realize this fact, or worse yet, tell themselves they are not creative. This forms a tremendous obstacle, because to be creative we must try, and this mindset keeps us from even attempting to think creatively. It becomes a self-fulfilling prophecy. Again, leaders have a role: to empower people to have faith in their own creativity.

The third and final approach to enhancing creativity involves a concept called "shifting paradigms." This idea is expressed in a book by Joel A. Barker entitled *Future Edge: Discovering the New Paradigms of Success.* Barker also discusses the concept in a film entitled *The Business of Paradigms,* which is widely used in organizations today for creativity training. Here is a brief explanation of the concept.

A *paradigm* is any set of rules and regulations (including procedures, standards, or routines) that guides you in solving problems. The paradigm establishes boundaries and it tells you how to be successful by solving problems within those boundaries. So paradigms can be helpful.

However, paradigms can also be the enemy of creativity, particularly when you try to discover the future by looking for it through old paradigms. They tend to filter out incoming experience. Inappropriate paradigms can actually blind you to new ideas and prevent you from seeing new ways to solve a problem.

Two examples may help you see the value of shifting paradigms. The first example is personal, the second is organizational:

Example 1. Picture the parents of an excellent high school student concerned about college costs. Some of the typical paradigms (rules) that can get in the way of creative solutions to their problem are:

- College must be "away."
- College must be attended immediately after high school.
- College must be completed in four years.
- College must be full time.
- One must stay at the same college for all four years.
- Average students always pay full tuition.

Changing some of these rules opens up such possibilities as attending local colleges or community colleges, innovative work-study arrangements, and the productive pursuit of scholarship assistance.

Example 2. It is no secret that the Catholic church has, for many years, seen a steady decrease in candidates for the priesthood. Many attribute this problem to a paradigm that says: no women priests and no married priests. Changing that paradigm would obviously change the nature of the problem.

Of course, it is always possible to look at the implications of a paradigm shift and then decide not to change the paradigm—and that's OK. But failing to consider paradigm shifts carries a heavy creativity penalty: The organization intentionally limits its thinking.

To apply the concept of "shifting paradigms" to develop creative solutions to tough problems you need to ask, "What rules or regulations are getting in my way, and could changing those rules or regulations pave the way to a solution?" If the answer is yes, then you know what to do: Attack the rules!

Situation Revisited

Ed Ryan is angry with himself, mad that he can't get his arms around this problem. He calls in four sharp people from his executive team. The meeting heats up as Ed tells them: "We must move on this. The trustees will be all over me, and they will be right. I'm going to get a group together Saturday morning to brainstorm this. I'll have the admissions people there, but I want you guys too, and this list of six others. What do you think?"

"The six people you have on this list know nothing about admissions."

"I know. I want some outside views, fresh perspectives. These people may not know admissions, but they are smart and candid and they represent diverse constituencies: faculty, staff, students, and trustees."

"What do you want from us, Ed?"

"Ideas. New ideas, maybe wild ideas to start with, and lots of them. Anything to shake up the system, challenge the status quo. We can then sort through them and find the best ideas."

"And Ed, what are you personally going to do now?"

"Well, first I'm going to e-mail the whole bunch and tell them to forget about thinking conventionally or even worrying about feasibility. Just bring a lot of ideas to the table. Then I'm going to generate some ideas of my own that we can test at the meeting. Now, we've spent enough time on this. Let's all go do our homework for Saturday."

It's late Friday evening at Ed's house. The family is asleep. Ed is drinking coffee and making notes:

—Let's expand the geographical recruiting area.

—I know the admissions staff is limited, but maybe we could use people differently.

—What about having the admissions staff train selected faculty volunteers to handle some of the recruiting (e.g., college nights at high schools)?

—What about using alumni? Have the admissions staff train a bunch of alumni volunteers to cover college nights, host gatherings at their homes, etc.

—How about our students: Could we train some of them to extend our reach into the high schools?

Ed looks at the stack of creativity books he's been reading and smiles. "Yep," he thinks, "it works. I'm getting out of the box, changing the paradigm, challenging the rules. I'll be ready for them tomorrow. It's going to be a new day, a better day, a creative day."

Application

❑ Do you ever allow yourself to "remain in the box" or be "bounded by the dots" as you attempt to solve problems? If so, can you force yourself to break loose from such artificial boundaries? In solving problems do you allow your mind to range freely over possible solutions and to look at the problems in a variety of ways? If not, can you force yourself to develop this skill? Pick a problem now and do your best to look at it from another angle.

◆　◆　◆

❑ Do any of the five mindsets or obstacles to creativity inhibit your thinking creatively? If so, can you force yourself to ignore these obstacles? As an exercise, think of some of your recent pressing problems and try to identify occasions where any of the five obstacles have limited your creativity.

◆　◆　◆

❑ Think of one of your most difficult personal problems and ask yourself this question: "What rules or regulations [i.e., what paradigms] limit my ability to solve this problem?" Look for ways to change the rules and thus reframe the problem. Check your thinking by talking to some smart people on your team.

◆　◆　◆

❑ Resolve to use this process on future problems.

Bottom Lines

➤ Everyone has creative potential, but it is often not fully developed or used.

➤ Enhancing individual creativity is a matter of changing our mindset, recognizing our obstacles to creativity (including rules that inhibit us), and learning to reframe complex problems into a more manageable form.

➤ With thought and effort, you can achieve enhanced creative capacity, and you'll find it has enormous payoff in improved performance.

Time Management:
Spending Time Where It's Needed

Typical Situation

Jack Ward, regional sales manager for a large pharmaceutical company, looks up from his desk, rubs his eyes and notices the clock—5:40 p.m. Where does the time go? What a day, week, month he's had. Sales have been down, so he's been out with his sales force a lot: observing, assessing, advising. Office work has piled up. Due dates face him. But tonight he's got to get home. Little League practice (he's the coach). The weekend won't help now that he's just agreed to chair the parish council; and of course, the grass needs cutting. On the ride home he thinks: "How can I get control of my time, and my life?"

Central Ideas

Time is *the* critical executive resource. Thus, an essential executive skill is to manage time well, to make effective use of this limited resource. Time-management skills can be learned, and the time invested to learn them is returned over and over again in improved performance and reduced wear and tear on ourselves and others.

I suggest seven approaches to time management here:

1. Slimming or eliminating roles
2. Reducing time wasters
3. Scheduling time effectively
4. Delegating
5. Managing group time effectively
6. Managing meetings
7. Reflecting on time usage

1. Slimming or eliminating roles. Role analysis gives you the opportunity to map your life and manage time in a macro sense by slimming or eliminating roles. The process is simple. Take a large piece of paper and place a circle at the center representing yourself. Then extend lines out from that center to points representing your various roles. Make sure you include your roles in all life areas: career, family, friends, social, civic/community, self-development, recreation, and hobbies. Once you've identified all roles, redraw the diagram placing each role at a distance from the center reflecting its importance to you (the closest roles being the most important). For example, part of my role set is shown to the right.

Next, examine each role to see if you can slim it (do less in the role), or eliminate it. For example, in my role as committee member I might decide to slim the role by refusing to chair the committee, or I might decide not to run for reelection when my term is up, thus eliminating that role.

It is also important to look for roles where more time should be allocated. Yes, you heard me right! Time management is not just about saving time, it's about allocating time to the

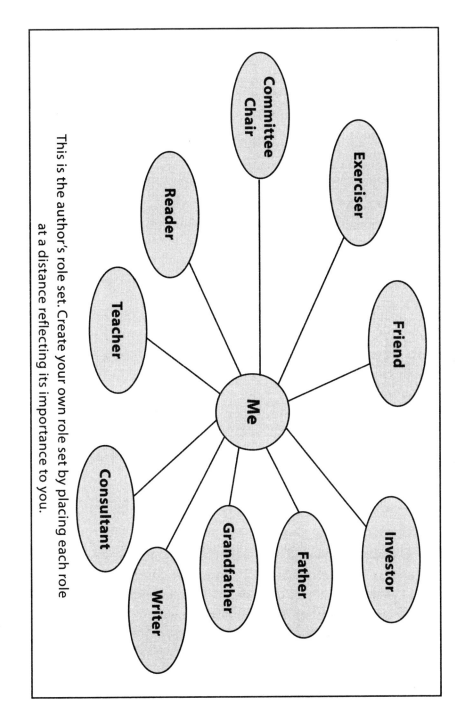

This is the author's role set. Create your own role set by placing each role at a distance reflecting its importance to you.

right things. Sometimes the role analysis will even reveal a new role, something of importance that we have been totally neglecting.

2. Reducing time wasters is an excellent way to micromanage your time by focusing on the little things that eat your valuable time. A typical set of personal time wasters might include:

- E-mail
- Unnecessary computer time (surfing)
- Interruptions (visitors, distractions, telephones)
- Involvement in too much detail
- Lack of priorities
- Meetings
- Paperwork
- Cluttered office
- Ineffective delegation
- Inability to say "no"
- Excessive socializing
- Travel
- Commuting
- Procrastination

Some time wasters can't be avoided. They may be an essential part of your life and work. For example, in my life, students frequently drop by to chat. Though this may interrupt something I'm doing, it is not a time waster. It is part of my job.

However, when you find a big time waster that you can eliminate or reduce, it can really make a difference in your life. For example, I once had a job where I traveled about two days a week by plane. Initially, these trips wasted a lot of my time.

But a friend made a great suggestion. He said the frequent business traveler should always carry with him three things: some fun reading material, something to study for self-improvement, and some work that can be done conveniently on the plane. I have always followed his recommendation, and my travels have been anything but time wasters.

3. Scheduling time effectively involves developing a convenient format for recording your schedule and adhering to certain guidelines for effective scheduling. The format should include the following elements:

—List of long-term projects
—Things to do this month
—Things to do this week
—Things to do today
—Schedule for today

Guidelines for scheduling time should include these principles:

—At the end of the day, prepare your next day's schedule to permit a fast start in the morning.
—Don't completely schedule your day. Allow time for unexpected events.
—Allow enough time for each scheduled event.
—Block off adequate amounts of time for major projects.
—Include all personal as well as professional events on your schedule (e.g., schedule your exercise time).
—Include some unscheduled thinking time for yourself, and time to relax and regroup.

Scheduling time effectively can't be overemphasized. We have to approach time scheduling with the same seriousness that we do the allocation of other critical resources. Further, because conserving time is so critical, I recommend you keep close personal control over your schedule. Think about it—when you let someone schedule your time, you give them control of your life.

4. Delegation saves time. It is also necessary to develop your people. So it is important to learn to delegate well.

The three major obstacles to delegation at work are:

- Our tendency to hold on to certain activities that keep us in the center of things (e.g., a briefing we give personally that provides critical organizational information).
- Our impatience when working through others. This can lead us to personally perform tasks that should be done by a subordinate.
- Our fear that subordinates will fail.

The first two obstacles can usually be overcome by changing your mindset or operating approach. The last (fear that subordinates will fail) can be addressed through training, either formal or on-the-job. One very effective approach to on-the-job training is to think of delegation as a continuum or range of actions in which we gradually increase a subordinate's involvement in some task. Consider the six steps below.

Step 1: Check into the problem. Report all the facts to me; I'll decide what to do.

Step 2: Analyze the problem. Let me know alternative actions, include pros and cons of each, and recommend one for my approval.

Step 3: Analyze the problem. Let me know what you intend to do; don't take action until I approve.

Step 4: Analyze the problem. Let me know what you intend to do. Then do it unless I say no.

Step 5: Take action. But let me know what you did.

Step 6: Take action. No need to contact me.

Each of the above steps represents some degree of delegation, and progressively moving a subordinate through the full continuum can be a powerful developmental experience. However, there's nothing sacred about these particular steps; they don't fit all circumstances. But the notion of gradually increasing a subordinate's responsibility for a task is always a useful delegation tool.

For example, I once had a job where I had to give a very complex and preparation-intensive weekly briefing to my boss and my staff peers. I happened to have a young subordinate with excellent briefing skills. I saw her as an opportunity to get this briefing off my back and at the same time give her some top-level visibility. But I wanted to be sure that she would perform well on her first appearance. So I gradually got her more and more involved in this briefing.

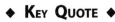

◆ **KEY QUOTE** ◆

"You can ask me for anything you like, except time."

—Napoleon

At first I simply had her do the research and update my briefing charts. Next, I had her brief me privately for a few weeks. Then I had her give the briefing to the full staff, but I rehearsed her first. Finally, I just turned the job over to her completely.

5. Managing group time is probably even more important to overall organizational performance than managing personal time, simply because of the large number of people whose performance might be adversely affected by faulty time-management practices. Often we thoughtlessly keep subordinates waiting, keep them too long in unnecessary meetings, or force them to abruptly change priorities. These and other dysfunctional things waste their time, and thus waste organizational time.

The best way to identify useful actions to effectively manage group time is to periodically ask subordinates two questions:

- What do I do that wastes your time?
- What can I do to help you use your time better?

A frank discussion of these matters can have a time-management payoff for the total organization. People will level with you if they know you are serious about making improvements (and have a thick enough skin to take a little criticism).

6. Managing meetings is extremely useful, since meetings can be huge time wasters for ourselves and others. Here are some meeting-management practices that I've seen helpful:

—Always ask yourself: Do we need a meeting, or can this issue be addressed without a meeting?

—Be selective in whom you invite to a meeting. Some possible attendees may not need to be present for the whole meeting. Consider inviting them to make a presentation of the information you need, then allowing them to leave the meeting.

—Be wary of regularly scheduled staff meetings.

—Send out agenda items well in advance of the meeting, with a brief explanation of each (e.g., "We must decide a course of action on this at the meeting," or, "I just want to update you on this and get a preliminary reaction."). Include any important reading material with the agenda.

—Establish in advance the starting and ending times.

To permit subordinates to plan their time, make it a practice to never run overtime. If more time is needed, schedule another meeting.

—Call or e-mail attendees to remind them of the meeting. This prevents everyone from waiting on one forgetful person.

—Be personally proactive in avoiding meetings that you feel you don't need to attend. For example, if you feel you were invited primarily because you have information of interest to the group, offer to provide your information in writing, or to give in a quick briefing, after which you leave.

7. **Reflecting on time usage.** The final approach recommended for any comprehensive time-management effort is to reflect on your use of time. We need to assess periodically how we are managing our time. A good technique is to occasionally think back through a very busy day and ask yourself: what went right, what went wrong, and how could I have made better use of my time?

Situation Revisited

Over the weekend Jack Ward picks up a couple time-management books—but, of course, he has no time to read them. Sunday evening he discusses his concerns with his wife. It's not news to her.

"Jack, I've been telling you this for years, and I worry about you."

"Any suggestions?"

"Yeah, take Monday off."

"What?!?"

"You heard me. Take a day off from work, from everything. Take your books to the park. Read them, and come up with an action plan."

"But I can't just take off."

"Yes, you can, one day. And when you come up with the right actions it will make all your days easier, better, and probably more productive. I'll play your mother—call in sick for you."

"It's worth a try."

Monday evening, mission accomplished (somewhat). Jack comes home for supper.

"How'd it go?"

"Pretty good. I did come up with some pretty promising ideas."

"Like what?"

"Well, here's my list:

—I'll never cut the grass again—that'll save me a half day or more every week.

—I've already asked Ted (assistant Little League coach) to handle half the practices. We don't both need to be there every time. He liked the idea.

—I intend to cut back on travel. Jim and Mary can handle many of the external visits. They might actually enjoy some travel, and I even think it would be good for new eyes to look at some of our problems.

—That parish council does not need to meet every week. It's been the custom, but it is absolutely unnecessary. I think others will agree. We all need more family time on Sunday.

"Enough Jack, I think you've got it. Great!"

Application

❑ Perform a complete role analysis of your life and work. Do you see any roles that should be added, slimmed, or eliminated?

◆   ◆   ◆

❑ Review the list of time wasters, and add any of yours. List your three biggest time wasters and write an action to help you avoid each of them.

◆   ◆   ◆

❑ Consider how you schedule time. Is your system effective for you? Do you adhere to the guidelines given here for scheduling time? If not, why not?

◆   ◆   ◆

❑ How would your subordinates rate you as a delegator: excellent, good, fair, or poor? What are the major obstacles that keep you from delegating?

◆   ◆   ◆

❑ What do you think your subordinates would tell you about how you could help them manage their time better?

◆   ◆   ◆

❑ Based on the meeting-management practices given here, how would you rate the meetings that you call: excellent, good, fair, poor?

◆   ◆   ◆

❑ Look back at your answers to the self-assessment questions above and try to identify your major personal time-management problems (e.g., too many roles, out-of-control time wasters, ineffective scheduling of time, poor delegation practices). Determine several specific actions that you can and will do to improve. Share your ideas with someone who works with you. Get their reaction. Then take appropriate action.

❑ Consider the issue of whole-life delegation. Is it possible to delegate something in one part of your life that will help you in another part? For example, by hiring someone to cut my grass regularly, I have been able to increase my consulting and recreational activities in the summer months.

◆ ◆ ◆

❑ Ask several key subordinates how you waste their time and how you can help them manage their time better.

◆ ◆ ◆

❑ At the end of your next meeting, ask each person to submit anonymously their best suggestions for improving organizational meetings.

◆ ◆ ◆

❑ For one full week, reflect back on each day and determine how you might have managed your time better.

Bottom Lines

➤ Nothing has a greater payoff, in reduced stress and improved personal efficiency, than better time management.

➤ Helpful approaches to managing time include examining roles and time-wasting activities, wisely scheduling time, delegating more, examining your handling of group time and meetings, and periodically reflecting on how you use your time.

➤ Learning to use these approaches is not difficult—and the return is time saved, over and over again!

Stress Management:
Rolling with the Punch

Typical Situation

Mary Turner, assistant V.P. of a regional bank, walks into her office, ten minutes late (again) for the morning staff meeting. The new child-care arrangement isn't working out well. Her daughter, Kelly, doesn't like the new sitter, and the location is all wrong for Ned (her husband) to take her occasionally. The days start out hectic and don't get better. No time to exercise anymore, boring business lunches that eat up time, always running behind on work. Then as the day ends, on to the sitter, the store, try to get dinner together. At night often irritable, too tired to sleep. Stress has a lock on her. What can she do?

Central Ideas

Stress is caused by three emotions: fear, anger, or sadness. The bad news is that you can't avoid some stressors. They will always be part of life. What's important is how you react to them. You trigger negative responses when you doubt your ability to cope with what life presents you. The good news is that we all have available to us many approaches to help reduce the harmful impact of stress.

On the next page is a descriptive model for an integrated stress-management program. It identifies major sources of stress and some of the typical coping mechanisms. Take time to study this diagram.

◆ KEY QUOTE ◆

"Learn to let go. That is the key to happiness."
—The Buddha

Stress has professional consequences in that it alters performance, usually in a negative way. It also has personal and social consequences causing illness, divorce, and sometimes crime. Yet stress is an inevitable part of life. The key is not to avoid stress but to learn to recognize your own personal stressors and to develop coping mechanisms that will help you deal with unavoidable stress.

There is a lot of literature available on coping techniques. Here is a sequence of three steps that have been helpful to me, and that I have seen work for others.

- *Self-Monitoring.* Lie down and get comfortable. Then mentally scan your body head to toe. Become a witness to your own stress responses by reflecting on any tension and on your emotions: fear, anger, or sadness.
- *Detach.* Try to make a sudden break with the stressful situation by saying to yourself: "Stop!"
- *Meditation/Deep Relaxation.* Slow your breathing, and count your breaths from ten to zero several times. Then again scan your body head-to-toe, first tensing then relaxing each part of the body. Let yourself feel

Integrated Stress Management Program

Sources of Stress

Work Setting
- Heavy Workload
- Time Pressure
- Goal/Role Ambiguity
- Political Climate
- Lack of Feedback

Personal Situation
- Feeling Alone
- Poor Health
- Low Physical Fitness
- Worry
- Physical Pain

Home Setting
- Marital Problems
- Problems with Children
- Problems with Relatives
- Illness in the Family
- Financial Problems

Stress Reducers and Coping Mechanisms

Exercise and Nutrition
- Diet
- Vitamins
- Walking
- Biking
- Running
- Swimming
- Team Sports

Support Systems
- Family
- Friends
- Pastor
- Doctor
- Team

Improved Professional Skills
- Goal Setting
- Role Clarification
- Time Management
- Delegation
- Team Building

Self-Awareness
- Awareness of Stress
- Self-Assessment:
  - Who am I?
  - How do I fit in?
  - What do I want?
  - What can I do?

Relaxation Techniques
- Time Alone
- Talk with Others
- Meditate
- Massage
- Yoga

inert (heavy or like jelly). Finally, focus on a pleasant thought, place, or image.

One other thing that has proven helpful to many is to develop some of the following habits of stress hardy people:

—Recognize your unique stressors.
—Don't let problems in one life area spill over to other areas.
—See troubles as temporary ("This will pass").
—See meaning in troubles.
—Focus on immediate matters ("What do I do right now?").
—Don't "awfulize." Ask: "What's the worst that can happen and how likely is that?"
—Ignore others' "shoulds"—as in, "You should . . ." Turn inward. Trust yourself.
—Know you are not alone. Take consolation from knowing others face similar or worse problems.
—Trust you can cope. Seek options. Don't get trapped.
—See the opportunity in troubles.

Focusing on stress-hardy characteristics and practicing the coping techniques above are good places to start. But I recommend you go beyond this. Buy a good book on stress management and experiment with the variety of techniques you'll find there. If you do that, I am confident that in short order your life will change for the better. And, while you're at it, think about the things you do that create stress for others. Acting on some of those findings will im-

◆ **KEY QUOTE** ◆

"Courage is the price life exacts for granting peace."
—Amelia Earhart

prove the lives of those around you and possibly improve both your family life and your organization.

Situation Revisited

Mary knows there's a lot she can do about her stress. Her friend, Joan, teaches stress management at a local college. They had a good talk. Joan gave her some things to read.

Now, heading for the airport on Wednesday for a business trip, she's determined and optimistic: I'll have two long plane rides and two nights alone at the hotel. Thinking time. I'll figure it out, get a grip on it.

◆ **KEY QUOTE** ◆

"There is nothing either good or bad but thinking makes it so."
—William Shakespeare

Friday night Ned meets a "new" Mary at the airport.

"You look different, Mary."

"How so?"

"Relaxed?"

"I am relaxed, but not as relaxed as I'm gonna be."

"So it worked."

"Yep. Simpler than I thought. Let's get home. Tell you later."

Friday night they sit up late. Mary tells her story:

"You know, Ned, I've been crazy, and dumb too. I really used the free time on this trip to think it out. First off, my situation is pretty typical. I took a look around the plane and picked out a dozen women that I bet have the same stress problems I do, probably worse in some cases."

"Why worse?"

"Because I had a chance to count my blessings. I, we, have it very good: good marriage, great kid, enough money, nice home, good friends. My stress problems are all work related, and I'm going to solve them at work."

"Tell me more."

"Well, Monday I'm informing them I'm going on flex time, coming in an hour later. That will give me time to take Kelly back to her old sitter who she loves. They won't love that at work, but you, Kelly, and I will. That's what counts. Also I'm going to stop saying yes to every request thrown at me. A big stressor for me is work overload, and it's my own fault. I say yes to everything. With the time I create I'm going to take a swim at noon every day. Pool's right in the building. I use to do it and loved it. But I got lured into the "let's have lunch" trap. Career enhancing maybe, boring definitely! That too changes next week. Get the idea?"

"I love it. And I'm proud of you."

"If it doesn't pan out at work, you can support me."

"You bet."

Application

❏ Examine the following list of typical warning signs of stress:

-irritability   -impatience   -difficulty concentrating
-fatigue   -headache   -daydreaming, preoccupation
-anxiety   -nervousness   -short temper & anger
-upset stomach -difficulty sleeping
-doing more or less eating or drinking

What are your top three warning signs? How do you react to them?

◆   ◆   ◆

❏ We can be stressed by many different things, including:

—time deadlines
—family difficulties

—poor work or attitudes of subordinates
—poor interpersonal relationships
—fear of failure or tasks beyond our ability
—lack of information
—surprises
—new job demands
—frequent moves
—multiple top priorities
—frustration at not being able to change "the organization"
—special life events: divorce, vacations, illness

What are your top three stressors?
In what environment (home or work) and under what circumstances do they occur?

◆　◆　◆

❑ Some of the most effective approaches in controlling stress are:

-physical exercise   -change in a routine
-talking to someone   -rest
-developing a plan   -quiet time/private place
-confronting the problem -reflection
-doing something pleasant -being with family
-self-imposed cool-off

What things do you habitually do when experiencing stress that seem to aggravate the situation? What three things could you do to reduce your stress?

◆　◆　◆

❑ Give yourself a stress check-up each month for a while. Ask yourself the following questions:
　—What are my personal and professional goals?

—Are my goals realistic?

—Am I using my time, energy, and resources appropriately to achieve my goals?

—Am I trying to do too much?

—What stressful events, disappointments, or losses have I experienced recently? What problems have I experienced with my work or relationships?

—How have I reacted?

—What coping mechanisms have I used?

—Have I been coping adequately?

—What more could I do to cope?

—How can I become more stress hardy?

Bottom Lines

➤ Stress can come from many sources: work, home, other personal situations.

➤ Sometimes professional help is needed. But often self-help is sufficient.

➤ There are many stress reducers and coping mechanisms: exercise, nutrition, relaxation techniques—all can be learned fairly easily.

➤ Self-assessment and the determination to act are key to reducing stress.

Life and Career Planning:
Deciding What You Want— And How to Get It

Typical Situation

Ellen Myers, a senior research scientist at the National Institutes of Health, was walking the beach at Ocean City, Maryland— just getting away for a few days to unwind and think. There was lots to think about. Her daughters were off at college. Her husband was engrossed in learning a new job as a result of his recent promotion. And she had just been offered a chance to move into a management position at NIH. She should be thrilled, but she wasn't. Something didn't fit. Just before this new job offer she had been considering an offer to teach science in a local high school. She was excited but uncertain. It would mean some big changes: pay cut, loss of perks, a change in professional status— but also a more relaxed lifestyle, more free time, no commuting, and the excitement of trying something very new, something she'd always dreamed about. As she walked, she wondered: "What should I do—and how do I think my way through this?"

Central Ideas

Life and career planning deserves a place in any discussion on managing yourself. The other topics in this section focus on how we think and manage. Certainly it is equally important to focus on the overall direction of our life and career, and in the process consider what we manage and even whether or not we should manage at all.

Many books on the market today describe how to do life and career planning. If you want to get deeply into such an exercise you would do well to visit your local bookstore to find a workbook that appeals to you.

My purpose here is to emphasize the importance of a periodic assessment of where you are headed in life and career, to spark your interest and possibly move you to action. A good friend of mine once told me: "If you don't think about where you are going, you will probably end up someplace else." His message is that we should be deliberate and systematic in planning our life and career, even while being a bit philosophical about all the uncertainties that can impact our plans.

There are three facts of life that I think ought to guide you in your pursuit of the right life/career direction:

- You are in charge of your life and career. So you must take charge of the planning. No one will care as much about the outcome as you do.

- It is possible to get so busy, running so fast, that you forget to ask whether you are headed in the best direction.
- Life and career planning won't happen by accident. You must have a system for doing it and you must allocate the time. But it is not rocket science. Ordinary people can deal with it, without outside assistance in most cases.

What follows is a fairly simple planning method. It may not prove to be totally sufficient for your final determinations. But it should generate enough ideas to let you know if more detailed analysis and planning are necessary.

On the next page you will find a descriptive model for use in the self-assessment process. It leads you from a look at your past and the events that have influenced you, to broad life goals. You are then asked to filter your broad life goals through five issues or factors:

—Values you want to actualize.
—Peak experiences you'd like to have.
—Things you'd like to start doing now.
—Things you'd like to learn to do well.
—Things you'd like to stop doing.

The purpose of this filtering is to help you decide on more specific life and career goals (supporting, of course, your broad life goals). Note that the specific life and career goals have two components: what you want to be, and what you want to do. This is an important distinction. What you want *to be* can be thought of as the job title you are seeking. What

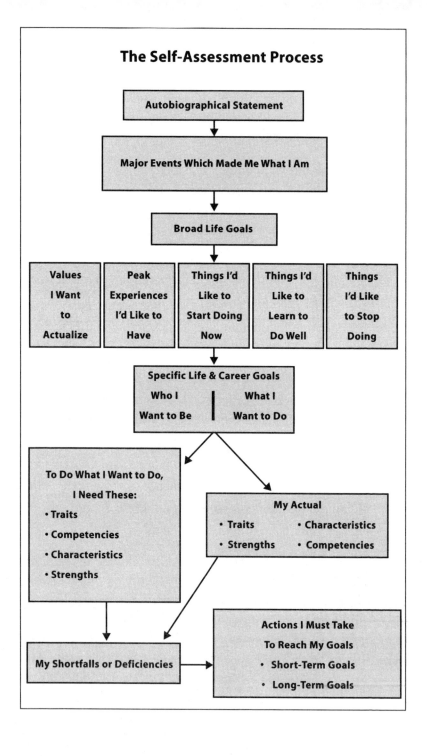

The Self-Assessment Process

Autobiographical Statement

Major Events Which Made Me What I Am

Broad Life Goals

| Values I Want to Actualize | Peak Experiences I'd Like to Have | Things I'd Like to Start Doing Now | Things I'd Like to Learn to Do Well | Things I'd Like to Stop Doing |

Specific Life & Career Goals

Who I Want to Be | **What I Want to Do**

To Do What I Want to Do, I Need These:
- Traits
- Competencies
- Characteristics
- Strengths

My Actual
- Traits
- Characteristics
- Strengths
- Competencies

My Shortfalls or Deficiencies

Actions I Must Take To Reach My Goals
- Short-Term Goals
- Long-Term Goals

you want *to do* refers to how you want to spend your time. Often these two things are in conflict, and without proper reflection you may find yourself in pursuit of a job that doesn't allow you to spend your time as you would really like.

The bottom line is this: You should let what you want to do influence what you decide you want to be.

Once having decided on specific life and career goals, the model suggests a competency analysis—comparing your actual resources to the traits, characteristics, strengths, and competencies required by your goals. This enables you to pinpoint any shortfalls or deficiencies and identify action plans to remedy important deficiencies.

> ◆ **KEY QUOTE** ◆
>
> "Whatever you can do, or dream you can, begin it. Boldness has genius, power and magic in it."
> —**Johann Wolfgang von Goethe**

Situation Revisited

Ellen was smart. Not just about science. She was smart enough to sense she should do some planning, and she had good instincts about how to proceed.

As she sat on the beach she began to fill her ever-present journal with ideas. Her thinking is reflected in the following journal notes:

—I don't think I'd be good at managing. Don't like to direct others or depend on their performance.

—I suppose I could learn. But why? I have never wanted to be a manager.

—I guess I want to be like my mother. She was a college professor and enjoyed it so. She loved her discipline (history), and her students. She also relished the freedom she had to pursue all kinds of interests. She always had that list of summer projects posted on the fridge. Never got it all done, but was always chipping away.

—I want that kind of freedom. I certainly know I want to get off the kind of work treadmill I'm on. I'd like to get back into distance swimming—really get in good shape. Need a different kind of job to do that.

—The high school job may be the answer. I need to talk to them in more detail.

—But I also like doing research. Maybe a college teaching position would be a better fit for me. I've got a lot of contacts at local colleges. Check that out.

◆ **KEY QUOTE** ◆

"I always wanted to be somebody, but I should have been more specific."
—Lily Tomlin and Jane Wagner

Ellen closes her journal. She thinks: "Enough for now. I have made one very important decision: to turn down the NIH management job. That was easy. But I have a lot of thinking to do about my next move. People to talk to, options to explore, timetable for actions. The NIH offer was a blessing though. Jogged me out of my complacency."

Application

❑ Using the self-assessment process, spend about an hour doing a crude job of sketching out ideas for each box of the diagram on page 64. Don't strive for comprehensiveness. Just generate some tentative ideas for each box.

◆   ◆   ◆

❑ Review your initial assessment each day for several days, and each time try to make some improvements. Keep working on your assessment until you can make a judgment about the following question: Do I feel that doing a comprehensive job of life and career planning might lead to some important new directions in my life? If the answer is yes, proceed to the next application steps.

◆　◆　◆

❏ Presumably you have now decided to pursue your life and career planning in more detail. Having revisited the descriptive model several times, I would expect you are now in need of additional assistance or input to progress further. My suggestion is that you visit a good bookstore and purchase a life and career planning workbook. There are many such books. A very good one is *What Color is My Parachute?*

◆　◆　◆

❏ Progress through the workbook in several sittings, never spending more than an hour at a time. After completing the workbook, put it away for a week (taking a break from this kind of work seems to enhance one's insights). After the break, go back through the workbook again, trying to improve on your analysis.

◆　◆　◆

❏ With the insights gained from the workbook, revise your original analysis, again using the descriptive model as a guide. Your instincts should be sharper now. You will be able to do a better job with the model. It is important to return to the model because it will force you to confront your initial thoughts again. The model will also force you to think of specific actions to achieve your goals.

◆　◆　◆

❏ When you finish your more refined work with the model,

share the information with someone who knows you well, to get validation that you are being realistic in your thinking.

◆   ◆   ◆

❑ At some point, before implementing any plans, have your plans reviewed by significant other people whose lives may be affected by what you do.

Bottom Lines

➤ It is important to rethink our career direction from time to time as our values, interests, and life situations change.

➤ Often we are so caught up in our current career and activities that we don't pause to see if we are going in the right direction.

➤ We need to stop, look, and listen:

—*Stop* long enough to reflect.
—*Look* at new possible futures.
—*Listen* to our significant others and to our own hearts.

➤ Fortunately, there are some excellent resources available (some in this module) to assist us in the search for direction.

Part Two

Managing Others

Motivation:
Getting People Moving—
In Right Directions

Typical Situation

Tom Elliot is perplexed. A plant manager for a large automobile tire manufacturer, he'd always prided himself on his ability to motivate people. He'd hire good people, turn them loose on problems, and watch them get excited about their work.

Dottie Abrams was one of his best. Hired two years ago as director of human resources, she'd hit the ground running and never stopped. Always upbeat and ahead of Tom, she ran on her own power, never needing advice or assistance—until about two months ago when things really changed. All her enthusiasm seemed to leave her, and with it her attention to her job.

She's now taking up a lot of Tom's time. Riding home one night, he gets angry, thinking: "What's wrong with her? The job's the same; I treat her as I always have, and as I treat everyone. What should I do about this? I have the weekend to think it over, but next week I have to do something."

Central Ideas

Motivation is the force that directs a person's behavior or activities toward goals. The motivational task of managers is to provide the necessary incentives so subordinates will direct their activities toward organizational goals.

One of the first steps in this process must be to determine the type of subordinate we are trying to motivate. Is this person a self-starter who seeks responsibility? Or are we dealing with a person who needs a good deal of push, control, or direction? To provide optimum motivation we must set an overall work climate that meets the subordinate's needs: enough freedom for the self-starter with strong initiative, and enough task direction for the person who lacks either ability or willingness to do the job.

I have found that most managers are helped by two classical motivational theories:

- *Maslow's Hierarchy of Needs*—useful in helping determine a person's motivational needs.
- *Expectancy Theory*—useful in helping design appropriate incentives to motivate someone.

In 1942, Abraham Maslow developed his **Hierarchy of Needs** theory. In it, he argued that man is a "wanting" animal. When one set of needs is satisfied another appears in its place. Satisfied needs do not motivate. Maslow arranged man's needs in a hierarchy of importance as follows:

—Self-actualization (highest)
—Esteem
—Social
—Safety

—Physiological (lowest)

Physiological needs are basic life-support needs: enough food and shelter. *Safety* needs include job security. *Social* needs are affiliation related: the need to be involved with others, to be a part of a team. *Esteem* needs cause a person to wish to be well regarded by others, to be respected by bosses, peers, and/or subordinates. Finally, the person motivated by *self-actualization* simply enjoys the work itself; doing the work is its own reward.

♦ **KEY QUOTE** ♦
**"Man acts from motives
relative to his interests;
and not on metaphysical
speculations."**
—Edmund Burke

The idea usually associated with Maslow's theory is that the lower-level needs must be satisfied first. Only then would a person be motivated by the upper-level needs. This is fine, as far as it goes. However, the reality is that most people are moving up and down the hierarchy all the time. As bosses, it is often hard for us to recognize this movement. The causes of movement often occur off the job and are personal in nature, but they impact the person's job motivation, so managers must be tuned in to any changes.

For example, you might have a great subordinate, a self-starter, who loves his work and is eager to accept any new task you assign. So you just keep giving him tough assignments and expecting outstanding results. But what happens if things are going poorly at home for that person due to illness, a child in trouble, a marriage falling apart, or financial difficulties? That person may suddenly move from self-actualization to the physiological or safety levels. He is not excited about the job anymore. He is worried about himself and his family.

What happens? Well, if you are a truly reflective manager, you may notice a change in performance, inquire about causes, and recognize the need for a new motivational approach. But too often we are not reflective, and don't wake up until something important doesn't get done right.

Maslow's Hierarchy of Needs is a useful framework to help keep you focused on the motivational needs of each of your people. Then you're in a position to act appropriately—and before a crisis in performance occurs. Also, managers often try to motivate all subordinates with the same incentives. Maslow shows us the folly of this approach. Motivation is a very particularized matter. You must tailor actions to each person's needs of the moment to be fully effective.

Expectancy Theory can help you design your actions to motivate someone. The idea is simple:

- First, determine the behavior or action you want from the other person.
- Second, determine some outcome that the other person wants. This outcome may not even be related to your own goals.
- Third, convince the other person that doing what you want is necessary for him to achieve his own desired outcome.

Let me illustrate this with a brief personal example. As a college teacher, I want my students to attend all class periods, but I don't like to be punitive by taking points away if they miss class. I want them to develop the sense of responsibility to attend on their own. To apply expectancy theory I must determine the outcome desired by my students—

normally, a good grade in the course. My motivational task is to convince them that to get what they want (a good grade), they must do what I want (attend class regularly).

I accomplish this by telling them that I do not teach from the textbook, that every day I will be putting them through learning experiences in class that are essential for a good grade. Then I make sure that my first test proves my point: you can't pass my tests without attending class. Most get the message quickly. My class attendance is always very good. I have motivated my students to be present by convincing them that they won't get what they want (a good grade) unless they are present.

Another point on motivation, something we often miss, but which can offer great motivational opportunities: our capacity to make work exciting for people. Excitement can be a great motivator for many people. It can often totally change the attitudes of some less-enthusiastic people.

Sports serve as a good example. Coaches make use of the technique all the time. I will admit that some kinds of work and certain kinds of organizations make it easier to generate excitement than others. But sometimes, even in a business or organization that is fundamentally unexciting, we can generate excitement in our part of that organization. When successful, the payoff is tremendous—so it is always worth a try.

I saw excitement pay off as a motivator some years ago in the U.S. Army. I had been assigned as chair of the Management Department of the U.S. Army War College, a ten-month, graduate-level educational experience for about 250 competitively selected army lieutenant colonels.

My management faculty consisted of fifteen army colonels. I was also given enough funding each year to hire two visiting civilian management professors. After a year of experiencing this system I went to our commandant and said: "I'll give you back half the money allocated for civilian professors if you will let me spend the other half each summer to send five of my military faculty to one of the four-to-six week, prestigious executive-management programs at various universities around the country." He agreed, and after two summers we had put ten faculty through programs at such places as Cornell, the University of Virginia, and the University of Pittsburgh.

The depth of knowledge and diversity of ideas brought back into our program were a great bonus. But the motivational impact was even greater. My people were truly excited by this new opportunity, and it had a tremendous impact on performance. It made me a believer. Excitement is a motivator!

One final point on a controversial motivator: money. Money is often considered a physiological motivator (in Maslow's hierarchy), and to some extent it is. A person without the means to satisfy basic needs will certainly be motivated by money to meet such needs.

However, the motivational impact of money can be more complicated than that. Money is more than just a means to satisfy basic needs. It can increase one's social standing, an important motivator to many. And, importantly, money is always an indicator to individuals of how much the organization values them.

People also want to be paid fairly within the organization's pay structure. Forget this and you'll soon see the motivational impact. I learned this the hard way. As chair of the Business and Economics Department of my college I needed to hire an accounting faculty member. One person I interviewed was ideal: a senior partner in a local accounting firm with years of successful part-time teaching experience who wanted to teach full time. He did not need our money. He'd made plenty and would continue a part-time affiliation with his firm.

But I made the mistake of offering him much too little by way of starting salary and title, and it offended him. He literally walked out of my office without comment. My offer said that we didn't value him very much, and he reacted accordingly. The lesson: Money motivates!

Situation Revisited

It's noon on Saturday. Tom and his friend Carl are relaxing after their traditional weekend tennis match. Carl's a good listener and a good head. Tom unloads his Dottie problem on him. Carl, ever anxious to toy with a problem, bores in.

"Nothing's changed for her at work?"

"Nope."

"No new responsibilities, subordinates, reporting structures?"

"Absolutely no changes."

"Could she be getting bored?"

"Hardly. She has challenges everywhere she looks."

"Pay?"

"She's well compensated here, and as HR director she knows that. We also pay well compared to outside firms. It's not money."

"Then it's a home issue."

"What kind?"

"That's for you to find out."

"How?"

"Ask her. You said you had a good relationship with her. She'll level with you."

"Think so?"

"Know so—do it!"

It's Monday, 3:00 p.m., Tom's office. It didn't take much to get Dottie to talk about her problem. Tom knew her husband was in the military but did not realize he had recently left for a one-year overseas assignment. And her parents, who had helped with child care, just moved to Florida. Dottie couldn't put it all together— big job, plus arrangements for three small kids. She was totally stressed out.

"Dottie, you should have told me."

"It's my problem, Tom."

"No, Dottie, it is our problem, and we'll solve it."

"How?"

"For starters, let's think how a more flexible schedule with some work done at home might help."

"I didn't think, as a director, it would be possible."

"We'll make anything possible to help you through this."

"Very kind of you."

"Dottie, it makes business sense, too. I don't want to lose your expertise. Tell you what. You think this out. What sort of arrange-ment will make things work for you? Then come in and we'll fig-ure out how to do it. Be as creative as you want. If I can't do ex-actly what you want, we'll keep working the problem till it's solved. OK?"

"Great. You don't know how much I appreciate this, Tom. I'll come up with a plan that will have the least impact on the company."

Driving home, Tom feels pretty good about the whole situation. It's amazing how he let himself get blindsided. He thinks, "Never thought of looking into possible personal problems Dottie might be having. And it was all there for the asking. She seemed relieved to let it out. And she'll come up with something workable and be at full steam again soon. Another disaster averted!"

Application

❑ Think for a moment about your own personal motivation.

—Where are you personally, at this moment, on Maslow's hierarchy relative to your job?

—Have you ever found yourself at different places on the hierarchy? What caused this movement? Were the factors personal or job related?

—Consider the idea of Expectancy Theory. Have you ever been motivated to do something simply to obtain a personal outcome that you desired?

◆   ◆   ◆

❑ Write down the names of two of your more difficult subordinates, the two that you have the most difficulty motivating. Assess each person and your motivational approach, and develop an appropriate action plan.

—Is this person a self-starter who seeks responsibility, or is this a person who needs pushing, control, or direction? Am I treating this person appropriately, given my judgment about his/her initiative and ability? How might I change my approach to produce better results?

—Where is this person on Maslow's hierarchy? Am I sure that I know enough about his/her personal and work situation to be certain about this? Should I initiate a conversation to make sure?

—Do I know what this person wants (what desired outcome) in return for doing what I want? How can I make this person understand that achieving this desired outcome depends on doing what I want done?

◆   ◆   ◆

❑ What can you do to make work a bit more exciting for your people? Talk to them about your idea, get feedback—then act on it.

Bottom Lines

➤ To lead, you must be skilled in motivating people.

➤ No single motivational approach will work with all people, or with any one person all the time.

➤ An individual's motivation is often influenced by factors off the job. You must be alert to changes in motivation, and take action to investigate the reason.

➤ You need a range of motivational techniques, and the good sense to change your approach when necessary.

Leadership:
Setting the Course—
And Inspiring Followership

Typical Situation

Ken Trainer knows he has a leadership problem. Recently promoted from regional sales director to V.P. for marketing of a farm machinery manufacturer, his new staff seems unhappy and unresponsive. He had always led with a very hands-on style, always available to his people with advice and assistance.

But what worked with his young sales representatives clearly isn't working with this group of experienced marketing managers. He confides to his boss, his old mentor: "These people think they are smarter than I am." To which his boss replies: "They probably are, at least you ought to hope so." Alone now, Frank thinks, "He's right! So, what should I do?"

Central Ideas

I would like to divide the treatment of leadership into three parts:

- A description of the nature of leadership.
- How to set the climate for leadership within the organization.
- How to select appropriate leadership styles for specific individuals.

What is leadership? Well, I teach management, and I know it's a lot more than that. One can often manage effectively simply by assembling great people and being skilled at integrating their efforts. But to lead you must want to take the organization to higher ground. To do that you need two things: the capacity to develop a vision, and the qualities that inspire others to follow. In my view, both of these abilities are clearly within the grasp of a determined person. Neither requires even a passing acquaintance with brilliance.

Vision springs largely from knowledge, but it need not be one's own knowledge alone. Collaboration is essential—first because in today's world no one person is likely to have all the answers, and second because authentic collaboration builds commitment to the vision. But there's a catch to this. While the leader doesn't need to personally have all the answers, the leader does need to have a credible knowledge of the business of the enterprise. And that is a moving target today. The required knowledge is continually changing. Thus the critical skill is the capacity for continuous lifelong learning, to keep pace with change. Certainly that's feasible, but it does require effort.

Inspiring followership is a less tangible quality; but it is learnable, though it was not always thought so. A touch of history might help at this point. World War II was the event that changed minds about this. Prior to that war the dominant leadership theory was called the "Great Man Theory." The name alone suggests how wrong the theorists were. But they were wrong about more than gender, because that theory held that leaders were born, not made—that leaders could not be trained.

World War II changed that view. The nation had to train leaders on a massive scale, in a big hurry. The professors who would later write the books on leadership participated in this experience; and in the world of battleships, infantry platoons, and bomber crews, they learned a lesson held to this day: ordinary people can learn to lead.

So what is the key? How do we find out how to do it? Literally hundreds of books are on the market today offering answers, some claim "the" answer. I have read many of them and would encourage you to do the same. They can be very helpful. But when I try to synthesize the nature of leadership, I'm pulled back always to words I read many years ago by the military historian S.L.A. Marshall, who studied and wrote about leaders in every war from World War I through Vietnam. Consider his words on the qualities that inspire followership:

> Quiet resolution. The hardihood to accept risk. A willingness to share rewards with subordinates. An equal willingness to take full blame when things go wrong. The nerve to survive storm and disappointment and to face each new day with the score sheet wiped clean, neither dwelling on one's successes, nor accepting discouragement from one's failures. This is the essence of leadership. For these are the things that have enabled one man to draw others to him in any age.

When you take this passage apart, line by line, I think it

says it all. It is part mindset, part action. It speaks to self-lessness as the indispensable quality. I like it because it matches my experience. I've known many leaders—in the military, in business, in government, and in education. As I think about the really great ones, I find they differed greatly in such matters as intellect, temperament, energy, and charisma. But they all had the quality of selflessness. A more recent term, servant leadership (the leader as servant of the follower), says much the same thing. It is a tough standard, and it can't be faked. Good people will spot a counter-feit in a heart beat. But in my view it is totally available to any-one who wants it, and is willing to pay the price.

◆ **Key Quote** ◆

"Leaders are people who do the right thing; managers are people who do things right. Both roles are crucial, but they differ profoundly. I often observe people in top positions doing the wrong thing well."
—**Warren Bennis**

Thus far this discussion has been confined to defining and discussing leadership in general terms and specifying an ideal leadership climate—a climate characterized by col-laboration in building a vision for the organization, and self-less behavior to inspire followership.

What about leadership style? What is style, why is it im-portant, and how does the leader find the most effective style mix for dealing with subordinates?

Briefly, style refers to the amount of task concern and re-lationship concern the leader shows in dealing with subor-dinates. Style is important because the leader must meet the follower's need for task direction and relationship behavior. Some subordinates will need a good deal of pushing or task assistance; others will crave freedom to act independently. Some will need a nurturing or participative relationship with the leader; others will prefer to work with minimal leader contact. The leadership task is to find a style that produces the best results with each subordinate. It takes patience, a reflective attitude, and a willingness to abandon ineffective styles. It is therefore essential that the leader possess the ability to move among a wide range of styles.

There are a variety of leadership theories that have associated sets of styles. I'd like to suggest a framework of six candidate styles: Helper, Educator, Commander, Persuader, Participator, and Delegator. I'll briefly describe each style and discuss the setting where it is most appropriate.

● **Helper.** The leader assigns work but, when results are in doubt or progress is slow, intervenes quickly to pull back the assignment or assist in its completion in a major way.

This style will work you to death and it hurts subordinate development. But it is appropriate in situations where immediate action is necessary and subordinates are either unwilling to tackle the task or incapable of getting it done properly. Emergency and crisis situations come to mind as sometimes calling for this style.

● **Educator.** The leader assigns work, then coaches or provides access to training.

When time permits, this is the appropriate style with a subordinate who is very willing but lacks the skills to do the job. This style can build subordinate confidence and capability and set the stage for later delegation.

● **Commander.** The leader clearly defines the task, specifies how it is to be done, and supervises carefully.

This is often an unpleasant style for many leaders today.

But it is sometimes necessary with subordinates who are clearly able to do the job but are for some reason unwilling. They need a push, and this style provides it.

● **Persuader**. The leader goes to great lengths to explain why a task needs to be done, and sometimes why it must be done a certain way.

This is an appropriate style with subordinates who trust the leader and respect her expertise, but still like to know the "why" of objectives or methods.

● **Participator**. The leader allows subordinates to participate in decision making, action planning, and implementation.

In certain organizational settings, participation is the norm today. A college faculty is one familiar to me: The people believe they have something to offer and want to have a say. Any organization is likely to have some people who want this style—highly skilled subordinates who know or believe they have greater expertise than the leader in a given matter. Meeting this need with a participative style becomes imperative in such circumstances.

● **Delegator**. The leader assigns the task and allows the subordinate to complete it with little or no supervision.

This is an ideal style when it can be used. It demands a high-quality subordinate, someone willing and able to do the job. And it requires a leader who can acknowledge the excellence of the subordinate (some leaders can't) and who is willing to accept some reasonable variance in results achieved.

The leader who can only be satisfied by his or her own narrow definition of success would have difficulty with this style. But it is an important style for three reasons: It is the only style that will retain extremely well-qualified subordinates in knowledge-based organizations; it is necessary for institution building in all organizations; and, importantly, it conserves the leader's time.

What we need to do as leaders is develop a full range of styles. Most of us prefer one or two styles. That's OK. It might even get us by in some organizations. But to lead subordinates of wide-ranging abilities and varying degrees of willingness, the leader must have command of all

♦ **KEY QUOTE** ♦

"You learn to know a pilot in a storm."
—Seneca the Younger

styles. Some you may not need often, but when you do, you'll need them badly. The promising thing is that everyone has the capacity to use all these styles. All it takes is a recognition that the set of styles exists and the willpower to use the styles appropriately. You can do it!

Situation Revisited

Ken decides to get a second opinion. He drops by the office of John Edwards, the oldest and most experienced member of his new team.

"John, I'd like your advice. We've got a great group of marketing guys here, but I must be doing something wrong. Most of them seem ticked-off at me at lot. We are embarking in a really new direction. There's a lot to do. How can I get them aboard?"

"Open the door."

"What?"

"Take them into your confidence. Let them participate in setting the new course and in deciding how to get there."

"Do they think they are smarter than I am?"

"Some might. Most know you are a very capable guy. But they do feel they can help you, and they kind of resent the fact that you move so quickly without consultation."

"Why didn't you tell me that, John?"

"You didn't ask, and though I like you, I didn't know how you'd react."

Ken had the weekend to consider a new approach and arrived Monday morning ready to go: no abrupt changes, but a gradual move to a more participative style. He'll start with Mary Sims, one of the brightest. "She's smarter than me," Ken thinks, "and she knows it. And here she comes down the hall."

"Hey Mary, got some time today? I'm uncertain how to proceed on the Branson contract. I could really use your advice."

"Sure, I'll stop by this afternoon."

As Ken walked on, he thought, "She smiled! She knows. She'll spread the word, too. I'll soon have them all aboard."

Application

❑ On the diagram on the next page, indicate on a scale from zero to ten the degree to which you feel you have the capability to use each of the six leadership styles (zero means no capability; ten means an outstanding capability). Mark a point on each vertical line, then connect the dots with straight lines to produce your profile. Do you judge yourself to be unacceptably weak in the use of any styles? Could you force yourself to use those styles?

◆ ◆ ◆

❑ In establishing your vision for the organization, do you feel you involve others to the degree necessary to gain their full commitment to the vision? If this question was posed to three of your top subordinates, what do you think they would say?

	Helper	Educator	Commander	Persuader	Participator	Delegator
10						
9						
8						
7						
6						
5						
4						
3						
2						
1						
0						

❑ Consider each of your three most difficult subordinates (those who seem to present the most demanding leadership challenges). For each of them answer these questions:

—To what degree is this person both willing and able to handle his/her most demanding tasks?

—Am I using the most appropriate leadership style with each of these subordinates? What style changes might I make to achieve greater effectiveness?

After answering these questions, experiment with changing styles if appropriate.

◆   ◆   ◆

❑ Approach three subordinates with whom you have a very good relationship. Ask whether or not you involve subordinates enough in developing a vision and goals for the organization. Try modifying your approach, if appropriate.

Bottom Lines

➤ In many small organizational settings, we get by fairly well using one dominant leadership style, the style with which we feel most comfortable.

➤ But in large organizations, with diverse types of subordinates, we must vary our style to meet the needs of each individual reporting to us.

➤ Thus we must have a broad range of styles, apply them tentatively to each situation, be reflective in observing our results, and keep making style adjustments until we find what works.

Negotiation, Influence, and Power: Picking the Lock *vs.* Breaking Down the Door

Typical Situation

Joan Burns, president of a small college in northern New England, has made a decision. She is going to allow drinking on campus by students twenty-one years of age. The college has never allowed drinking. But the past two winters, five students (all seniors over twenty-one) died in accidents driving the twelve miles into town to party.

On-campus drinking will have its problems. But the problems are worth the risk. The question on her mind is how to do it. She could just use her power as president to force the change (i.e., "break down the door"). But it would be far better to find a softer way (a way to "pick the lock"). It's late at night. She's trying to design a strategy, but it's not coming. She's only able to jot down a few words and phrases—trying for a toehold:

—Negotiating climate (how tough?)
—Multiple constituencies (who?)
—Power—how much do I have/need?

—How to grease skids for this?

—Get advice/help!!!

Joan hits the sack—to worry, not sleep. "Tomorrow," she thinks, "back to brainstorming on this, big time!"

Central Ideas

The topics of negotiation, influence, and power are treated together here because all are aimed at one common purpose: to get your way.

- *Negotiation* is the overall process of dealing with another to get your way. The style of negotiation, soft *vs.* hard, sets the tone of the encounter and can impact the outcome.
- *Influence* is a strategy to so involve and educate someone about your point of view that, in the end, that person will want what you want. It is difficult to do; sometimes it's not possible. But there are ways to increase the probability.
- *Power* is the ultimate capacity to get your way. Your power depends on how others view your capabilities and qualities. They may do what you want because they respect your title, or recognize your special expertise, or simply because they are drawn to you by certain intangible qualities. However, they still may not be convinced that your way is the right way.

Negotiation. The important decision in setting a negotiation tone is one of style selection. Should we use a hard or soft bargaining style? Most people rightly see negotiation style as highly situational. To help them identify their style preference I like to ask managers to think of a typical negotiation situation, and in that context, complete the negotiation profile below.

Note that there are eight characteristics of soft negotiators on the left and eight corresponding characteristics of hard bargaining on the right. Later, I'll ask you to draw your own negotiating profile as part of a self-assessment exercise. For the moment, just note the variety of characteristics to be considered in making the hard *vs.* soft judgment about one's style.

Negotiation Profile

SOFT NEGOTIATORS		HARD NEGOTIATORS
Trust the other person	_____	Distrust the other person
Aim for agreement	_____	Aim for victory
Have flexible goals	_____	Have rigid goals
Disclose their bottom line	_____	Withhold or mislead regarding their bottom line
Make offers	_____	Make threats
Accept some losses to reach agreement	_____	Give no ground
Make concessions in order to preserve the relationship	_____	Insist others make concessions to sustain relationships
Yield to pressure to avoid a contest of wills	_____	Apply pressure to win a contest of wills

Influence. Let's next consider influence. Think of it as I defined it earlier: getting others to want what you want. It really is hard to do. I might be able to get you to do what I want for a variety of reasons. You might do it because you like me, or fear me, or perhaps because you respect my expertise. But you may not be totally convinced I'm right. In-

fluence is about being so persuasive that the other person finally
wants the same thing you want.
Influence is much softer than
power. With power you "break
down the door." With influence
you "pick the lock." Both help
you get your way. Sometimes
power is the only way to move forward. But it is always wise
to first try to influence.

The concept of influence involves four process activities,
three styles, and a series of steps for designing your influence plan (your plan to meet with the influencee).

The four influence process activities are:

- *Lobbying*: Identifying all the people you will need to
  talk to in order to accomplish your objective. You must
  also, in this step, decide on the best order to approach
  people. Failing to touch all key bases or touching
  them in the wrong order can spell disaster even for
  the best of ideas.

- *Negotiating*: The direct bargaining that takes place
  with each individual. This is where influence styles
  are helpful, as we'll see later.

- *Networking*: Using a third party to assist. This might
  be a person having a special relationship with your
  influencee, or it could be someone with recognized
  expertise, thus highly credible.

- *Assessing your constituency*: In this step you keep your
  eye on the degree of support you have. Assume you
  are going into a meeting to make a proposal to a group
  of people. Think about it. Wouldn't it be nice to know

in advance how many are on your side?

The three influence styles are: *logic*, *common vision*, and *mutual participation*. These styles are useful as categories to help us find specific arguments. They can be described as follows:

- *Logic.* The focus of this style is on getting the facts straight and doing the necessary cost/benefit analysis. This style relies heavily on logical arguments, accurate facts, and careful presentation of the evidence. In our culture this is always a necessary style. We tend not to respect people who do not do their homework. This is homework!

- *Common Vision.* This style must also rely on totally factual information and logical arguments. But the arguments are designed to appeal to the values of the influencee. Common vision arguments consider the hopes and aspirations of others—what they want for the organization, for other people, and for themselves. Such arguments target emotions and create excitement. It is important to cultivate this style because when dealing with visionary people, you must include common vision arguments as part of an overall influence strategy. Logic arguments alone seldom suffice.

- *Mutual Participation.* This style builds commitment through dialogue. You let others know you value their input and have the flexibility to consider that input in any solution. You take all the time necessary to explore alternative ideas. The goal of the discussion is a course of action both parties can live with, and both parties are committed to, because they created it jointly.

With the influence process activities and influence styles as tools, you are now ready to think through the development of an *influence plan*—a step-by-step process to develop your arguments. The process involves asking yourself these questions:

—Whom do I want to influence?
—What exactly do I want to happen at the first meeting? What is my objective for that encounter?
—What are the relevant characteristics of the other person? What about this person might provide a clue to the best influence approach?
—What influence styles should I use?
—What actual arguments should I use as I apply each selected influence style? Note that the styles represent categories of arguments. They help point you to specific arguments.
—What conflict do I expect? What do I expect the other person to say in rebuttal?
—How should I deal with this conflict?

At this point you may be thinking that I'm suggesting you use the influence techniques every time you meet with someone. Actually, I suspect that most of the time you will do what I do: forget all about your theory and just wing it! That's reasonable, most of the time. However, my conviction is this: When you have a really tough opponent, and a difficult issue to resolve, and you care a lot about the outcome—using the influence strategies outlined here will give you an edge.

An example from my own experience might serve to convince you of the usefulness of the influence approach. While in the army in the late 1960s, I was assigned to a staff position in which I was responsible for plans, training, and operations for a force of about 15,000 troops stationed in Europe. The commanding general to whom I reported was known to be extremely demanding. The Vietnam War was going full blast. All units in Europe were short of officers. My staff section was operating at one-third its authorized strength. My dilemma and my solution follow.

In my first month on the job, as I had been warned, staff meetings with the general were a nightmare. He was interested in every detail about the command and continually hit me with questions I could not answer and demands I could not meet. I liked this man, but I felt I was in trouble and that my troubles would deepen unless I could convince him to reduce his demands to a level I could handle with my available staff.

What I had was the perfect set-up for an influence effort. And my actions provide a good example of all three influence styles. I prepared a detailed briefing for the general which began: "The purpose of this briefing is to propose a course of action that will help me serve the command, and you, more effectively than I feel I am at this time." It was a common vision statement. And I could tell immediately that I had his attention. He was a good man. He liked me, which is why I had this job. It was not his nature to want to make my job difficult. But he was a hard worker, a very pragmatic manager, and very analytical by nature. Consequently, he had unlimited needs for information and staff assistance. My objective in

> ◆ **KEY QUOTE** ◆
> **"Unless both sides win,
> no agreement can be
> permanent."**
> **—Jimmy Carter**

that briefing was to negotiate an agreement for a workload I could handle. To do that I would have to first lay out the facts (logic style) then get him to participate in setting some priorities (mutual participation style).

I showed him a large chart on which I had listed all the things he'd seemed most interested in, the things he'd been asking me about. I stated candidly that, with the staff I had, I could not do a thorough job on all these things. I went to great pains to prove my point. For example, "Every Monday you ask me about the status of training during the past week. With only six officers, and over fifty company-sized units in the command, spread over hundreds of square miles, I can make spot checks of training, but not enough checking to provide you a reliable assessment of status."

Then I addressed all the items on the chart. I had written them in three colors: black, for those I felt I could do comprehensively; green, for those I could handle reasonably well but not have information immediately available; and red for those I felt I could do very little about (monitoring unit training was one of these).

Finishing my pitch, I watched him. He was thoughtfully studying the chart. Finally, he said: "John, I like this. Change the second green item to black and the last two red items to green and let's try to work with that. Also, keep this chart and bring it in here every week or two and we can make adjustments as needed."

I left. I'd gotten what I wanted. He'd slimmed down the job. And my life became much more pleasant. Staff meetings never again seemed even slightly adversarial. Once in a while he'd say: "Bring the chart in later today." The chart got revised, marked up, remade three times during the year I worked there. As I look at it now, this was a good influence effort. It ensured knowledge of the facts and cost/benefit issues: "This is my staff; you are asking for more than we can do." It was built on a common vision: "I want to serve the command effectively, just as you do." And it used mutual participation to accomplish the goal: "Let's work together to establish priorities."

Power. What about power? What is it, why do we need it, when and how do we use it? As mentioned earlier, power is the capacity to get your way. Influence won't always work. We can't always get people to actually want what we want. But to lead we must ultimately, in key matters, get our way. Power is the key to doing so. Power is not only one way—it is often the only way to move forward.

There are two kinds of power:

- *Position Power* causes others to give us our way because of our title (boss, father, mother, coach, teacher) and our related capacity to reward or punish.
- *Personal Power* causes others to give us our way because of their perception of our expertise, our charisma, or our connection to them or relevant others.

We see position power at work every day. Think about it. Don't you often give others their way because of their title? And don't you often get your way because of your title?

Let me illustrate position power by another personal example, in a situation that occasionally confronts all managers: an able employee who is performing well below his potential. I developed an approach that normally solved this problem in short order. After trying for a reasonable length of time to improve the person with verbal comments and suggestions, without success, I'd call him in and hand him a handwritten letter of reprimand. After he'd read the letter, I'd say: "No one has seen this except you and me. No one knows you are in trouble with me. This is the letter I'll have to send you if you don't get your act together. But I don't want to send it, and I'm sure you don't want me to. So, here's what you need to do to get back in good standing [I'd be very specific]. Do those things, and in three months we'll meet again. You bring your copy of the letter and I'll bring mine. I bet we'll be able to tear them up. I have confidence you can do a very effective job here, but these things have to change."

Normally, after a month or so I'd see a big change. I'd take my copy of the letter, walk up to the person, and say: "Here's the letter, I knew you could do it. Tear up both copies, and keep up the good work."

That was an example of coercive power, a type of position power. It's not pleasant to use, and I think it should be used only as a last resort. But, when you need this style, you often need it badly, and must use it in the interest of the organization and the individual. Though it seems a bit of a brute-force approach, I've seen it both save jobs and preserve individual dignity. Not a bad achievement.

Personal power is equally important and we find it at all levels of the organization:

—The helpful person, far down in the hierarchy, who has special information or expertise that everyone needs from time to time.
—The good networker with strong connections within or outside the organization.
—The charismatic person with a natural touch for leadership.

All of these individuals have power. Their ability to get

their way with others is independent of formal organizational title. They are a force to be reckoned with—and a resource to be used by institutional leaders.

Situation Revisited

Next day, Friday at 1:00 p.m. The brain trust assembles in the college conference room: provost, dean of academic affairs, dean of students, a senior professor and a nontenured one, two student leaders, director of admissions, director of alumni relations, president of the parents' council, and the director of campus security. Joan briefs them: "This is what I want to do, what I undoubtedly *will* do unless you convince me I'm crazy. But I don't want to make any final decision today. I just want to brainstorm the pros and cons, plus lay out the implementation actions sufficiently to help in conceptualizing a tentative strategy. Then I'd like to play with this alone for a week or so and present a tentative plan to you and let you help refine it—or maybe tear it apart. We'll see."

Friday, 4:15 p.m. Joan ends the meeting. As she thanks one and all for their input, she thinks: "Input, did I ever get it—half a steno pad filled with notes. I'm going home, sleep on it, and try to make some sense of it over the weekend, and plot my next moves."

Saturday. Joan goes over her notes and jots down some thoughts:

—Glad I got that group together. Taking them into my confidence made me some points.
—Plus, I got a lot of ideas.
—If we had taken a vote, the majority would have supported the idea, though a few certainly oppose the concept. Implementation worries many of us.
—Provost is my hardliner: "Why don't you just do it, you're

the boss." Naive as usual. Sure I have the power, but I need to bring the many constituencies aboard—educate them on the why and how. The way others jumped on the provost got his attention, makes my job easier with him.

—The head of the parents' council and the admissions director both feel I could run into opposition from parents of present and prospective students. They agree I'm right, but advise a strong educative effort. I can see I'm going to really need to lay out the facts and cost/benefit arguments. Gio (dean of students) offered to gather data from other colleges that allow drinking on campus. Hopefully that will help me build my case.

—The chief cop [director of security] worries about how to handle students under twenty-one. If I let him he'll turn us into a police state. Have to meet with him privately, and get him to work out an enforcement plan we can live with. I'll ask Gio to help with that—a voice of reason.

—Gotta brief the board of trustees early on this, even before I get near a final plan. I'll call the board chair on Monday, just give him a heads-up, get some advice on when and how to approach the board. Maybe I should meet with him instead of calling. I'll think about it.

—I'd better meet with Jon [dean of academic affairs] right away, Monday morning. He was pretty dysfunctional at the meeting. All that noise about this hurting our academic reputation, getting thought of as a party school. If I don't get him under control he'll have the whole faculty on my back. I'll use my power to prevent that: "Jon, I want you to take charge of getting the faculty behind this." Any static and I'll ... well, lets just first see how he reacts.

—I've got some good stuff going for me: The need to do "something" is obvious, and my relationship with the board is solid. Even the faculty (my strongest critics always) know I've made some good calls in the past on some tough issues. They trust me as a leader.

Joan puts down her pen. "Enough for now. I'm farther along than I was a few days ago. Some more private thinking tomorrow. It won't be easy but I'm a good negotiator. I have both a heavy hand and a light touch when I need them. I'll make it happen."

Application

❑ Turn to the Negotiation Profile on page 93. Consider the lines drawn between the soft and hard bargaining characteristics to be linear scales. Now think of some person with whom you negotiate a lot, and think of an issue about which the two of you negotiate frequently. For each pair of opposing characteristics plot a point on the line that best represents your attitude or approach. Your point may be on the left or right, or anywhere along the line.

After doing this for all eight of the characteristics, draw a series of straight lines connecting your eight points. That is your negotiation profile. The way to use the profile is to think about your position on each line, particularly positions that are far to the left or right. Is that attitude or strategy helping you in the negotiation process or hurting you? What changes could you make to improve your effectiveness? Are you fundamentally a hard or a soft bargainer? Which do you feel is most effective?

Personally, I've found that most of the really effective managers I've known have had a reputation for being easy to do business with. They were fundamentally soft bargainers, but (and it's a big but) they were people who could hard-bargain aggressively when necessary. People knew what part of their turf to respect and which of their values were sacred.

◆   ◆   ◆

❑ On the diagram at the top of the next page, indicate on a scale from zero to ten the degree to which you feel you have the capability to use each of the three influence styles and the degree to which you feel capable of using power to get your way (zero means no capability; ten means an outstanding capability). Connect the dots to create your profile.

Don't be discouraged if you feel forced to rate yourself low on certain styles. They are all important to master, but with a bit of effort you can force yourself to use all of them as the occasion demands.

◆   ◆   ◆

❑ In assessing your power, do you feel you get your way with subordinates mainly through position power (your title)? Or do you feel they give you your way mainly through respect for your personal power resources such as your expertise or your charisma? What do you think they would say if you asked them?

◆   ◆   ◆

❑ How would you rate your connection power to your superiors? Is there an atmosphere of warmth and mutual support? Could you do anything to improve the relationship?

◆   ◆   ◆

❑ Think of a very demanding future influence situation— some situation of importance to you, and one in which you

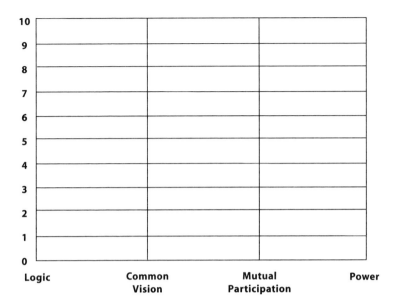

will need to deal with a difficult person. Using this situation as context, develop an influence plan for converting the other person to your point of view. Use the steps discussed earlier to guide you.

—Who is the influencee?
—What do I want this person to do?
—What are that person's relevant characteristics?
—What influence styles are most appropriate with this person?
—What actual arguments will I use (let the selected influence styles point you to arguments)?
—What do I expect the other person to say in rebuttal?
—How will I deal with the conflict?

Consider what kind of an overall negotiating climate will be most effective as you talk with this person. What soft bargaining or hard bargaining characteristics do you feel are relevant in this situation?

Put your influence plan into operation by actually using it to try to convince this person of your point of view.

Did you find that you had to resort to power at any time during the influence attempt?

Bottom Lines

➤ Senior leaders normally have a good deal of authority: the legitimate power to order things done. It's useful, often necessary in emergencies, but should be used sparingly.

➤ A softer negotiating style and efforts to influence through involvement, education, and appeals to others' values and emotions should normally be attempted first.

➤ When skillful influence efforts are successful, good will and commitment result. If they are unsuccessful, one can always exercise a power strategy as a last resort.

Managing
Interpersonal Relations and Conflict:
Capitalizing on Differences

Typical Situation

Bob Cole, director of production for a small electronics manufacturing firm, is upset. He was just about to leave for a meeting with Tim Wall, director of engineering, to divide up the resources for the Techtronics Project. And what walked in? One of Tim's "ultimatums." A memo outlining his resource needs. A preemptive first strike, as usual.

Bob settles down, reads the memo. He thinks: "He's got a good case here, very persuasive. I don't think he's padded it; he needs all this. But I have my needs, too. And the total's just too big. Ed [the President] gave us this target figure, and we'd be 20 percent over it. I've got my work cut out. Tim's memo sounds like he'll fight hard. He usually does. Compromise is not in his vocabulary, and I guess I agree he can't compromise on this. He's waiting. Maybe I can lead us all into a workable solution. Here goes!"

Central Ideas

Cultivating and preserving good interpersonal relationships and managing conflict are important for personal effectiveness at all levels of the organization. They are absolutely essential skills for leaders. Further, the absence of these skills at senior-management levels marks one as an unsophisticated performer, unsuitable for high responsibility. Good management eventually depends on successful one-on-one encounters, which are always influenced by relationships. And you rarely solve tough problems without confronting the differences in viewpoint that constitute conflict.

Good interpersonal relationships sometimes develop spontaneously: two people feel a mutual attraction. More often, however, we need to work at the problem of building and maintaining relationships. Here are a few suggestions that can help you in this effort.

● *Build a personal reputation for candor, honesty, and flexibility.* The word on such things spreads quickly and easily in organizations. Think about it. You're going to meet someone for the first time and take the time to inquire about her. A colleague says: "She's a straight shooter, reasonable to deal with, but says what she thinks and does what she says she will." You'd expect to like this person. Her reputation would get the relationship off to a good start.

● *Respect the other person and show it.* Perhaps the best way to show appropriate respect is to talk to the other person as an equal. One of the quickest ways to upset a relationship is to talk down to someone. No one likes that, and few will tolerate it. And it is something that's easily controlled. Even if (in the heat of an argument) the other person talks down to you, in the interest of preserving the relationship, you can refrain from responding in kind. You are always in control of what you say.

I once had a boss who was always trying to keep his subordinates off balance. If you went to talk to him about some issue, he'd typically turn on you and suddenly ask for status on unrelated projects, and keep digging until he found something to criticize. Often he'd really put you down: "This isn't on track because you've got your priorities wrong." When he talked down to me, I was always tempted to talk down to him in return: "You just don't understand this project." But, I never did that. Maintaining some reasonable relationship with this difficult person was too important to my overall ability to do my job. I'd just let it go, try to change the topic, get on some issue that was going well.

> ◆ **KEY QUOTE** ◆
>
> **"The understanding that underlies the right decision grows out of the clash and conflict of opinions and out of the serious consideration of competing alternatives."**
> —**Peter F. Drucker**

That example may sound like a phony gesture to feign respect, but I don't see it that way. Usually, people who act that way are personally insecure, not willful. And I've found if you look a bit deeper you can find some basis for respect (not always, but usually). Focusing on that can help you move forward in a positive way.

● *Seek to understand the other person, and the reasons for his opposing views.* Sometimes people see situations differently because they have access to different sets of data and information. Establishing agreement about the reality of a situation is a good first step toward mutual problem solving, which avoids unpleasant confrontations that upset relationships.

Recognizing that others have multiple roles can also help you understand their views. For example, assume you were

assigning a task requiring a great deal of travel to a subordinate. That person has a family problem requiring her pres-
ence at home every night. If that person reacted negatively
to the assignment, and you did not know the reason, it could
upset the relationship. And the person might not tell you
about the problem, or might assume you are already aware
of it. So—what's the solution? I think we have to question
people sufficiently to identify role conflicts that can lead to
views and attitudes that harm relationships. It's not easy to
do, but it can really help and is worth the effort.

In summary, bad interpersonal relationships lead to aggressive behavior, anger, distrust, and a dislike for one another. Once a bad relationship develops, it is difficult to re-
verse and impacts all dealings, even on issues where there
is general agreement. I'm not recommending that you never
take a harsh stand with someone. Sometimes, aggressive
treatment is deserved and appropriate. I am suggesting that,
in cases where preserving the relationship is important to
you, you go the extra mile to avoid bad relations. In such
cases, I think the techniques here will help.

Let's turn now to conflict, a good force that we need to
encourage. Conflict is merely a difference of opinion between
two individuals over a given issue at a given point in time. It
can be caused by lots of things: protecting turf, competing
for resources or rewards, or simply differences of opinion on
technical issues.

If an organization has difficult problems to solve and a
collection of talented people, conflict is inevitable. It is actually necessary for creativity. We need lots of diverse opinions to tackle tough problems. But conflict must be managed. The first step in managing it is to provide settings where

the various opinions can be heard, and to take care not to dampen conflict.

I once did a good deal of consulting with a firm that was a classic case of poor conflict man-
agement. They would actually wait until a couple of the "rebels" on the staff were out of town be-fore discussing controversial is-sues. And, when thoughtful people raised "embarrassing questions," they were often ig-nored or quickly dismissed with-out debate. Such bad practices cost that organization much in creativity.

> ◆ **KEY QUOTE** ◆
> **"Competing pressures tempt one to believe that an issue deferred is a problem avoided: more often it is a crisis invited."**
> **—Henry Kissinger**

Once conflicting views are aired there is still much to do to manage the conflict. It helps to think in terms of a set of five styles and select the style most appropriate to the situation.

- *Competition:* Used when we must get our way, and decide to fight if necessary to prevail.

- *Accommodation*: Used when we are willing to sacri-fice our own interests in order to let others win. We may want cooperation from them later in return, but at this time and on this issue we are willing to give ground.

- *Compromise*: Used when we can afford to give some ground, get part of what we want and allow others to meet some of their needs as well.

- *Avoidance:* Used when we want to temporarily sus-pend negotiations. No one wins at the moment. The conflict is to be resolved later. You might use this style to temporarily suspend negotiations until tempers quiet or until necessary new data can be obtained. However, it is important to note that you are not damping out the conflict, not suggesting it never be resolved. You are merely saying that no one wins at this particular time.

- *Collaboration:* Used when both parties to a conflict need to get fully what they are requesting. There is no give. If either fails to get what they want, some project fails. If the parties recognize the reality of the situation, they may decide to collaborate in developing a request for additional resources, so that they both get what they need.

This framework of styles provides a very effective strategy for managing conflict. It helps us see the styles being used by others. And it provides a set of five candidate styles for our own use. It also highlights an important reality about conflict: We cannot get our way all the time; sometimes we must give ground to others. A lot of people fail to recognize that and must be educated to that fact. This too is part of our job in managing conflict.

Situation Revisited

Bob walks into the conference room. Tim's there, looking aggressive as usual. He speaks first.

"Get my memo?"

"Sure did. I agree with you."

"You do?"

"Yep, but I'd like you to hear my story."

"I'm not backing down."

"I understand. But I read your memo, so let me tell you what I need. If you agree with me, I've got a suggestion on what to do."

[Tim nods; Bob briefs]

Tim speaks:"Persuasive. But that puts us way over budget."

"I know. But think about it. This project needs both of us fully participating. It will fail if either of us can't do our part."

"So, what do we do?"

"First, let's you and I not fight. Let's work up a new story for Ed. Propose a new budget. He cares a lot about this project. And he trusts us. He'll increase the budget if we both agree."

"Great. Let's get to work."

Bob thinks: "God, I can't believe it. He's actually listening to reason. First time. A winner!!"

Application

❏ On the diagram at the top of the following page, indicate on a scale from zero to ten the degree to which you feel you have the capability to use each of the five conflict management styles (zero means no capability; ten means an outstanding capability). Mark a point on each vertical line, then connect the points by straight lines to form your profile. Do you judge yourself to be unacceptably weak in the use of any styles? Could you force yourself to use those styles?

❏ Try to think of a bad interpersonal relationship that you have had in the past at work or in your private life that would have been helped by:

　—A greater appreciation for multiple roles (yours or the other person's).

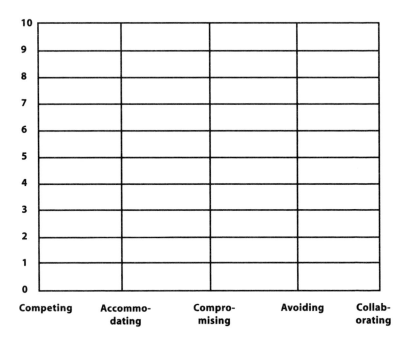

—One or both of you resisting the temptation to talk down.

—More exploration of the facts; a greater attempt to ensure a shared reality about the situation.

◆ ◆ ◆

❑ Think of a person with whom you have a very poor interpersonal relationship right now, one you'd like to improve. Using one or more of the three approaches above, develop a plan to improve your relationship with that person. Then put your plan into action.

◆ ◆ ◆

❑ Think of some person in your professional or personal life with whom you are currently in conflict over some issue.

Try to pick a person that you basically like and get along with (to avoid having to deal with both conflict and interpersonal relations problems simultaneously). What styles of conflict do you think the other person will be most inclined to use with you? What style do you think it would be best to use? Meet with this person. Try to use the appropriate conflict management style yourself, and gently attempt to move the other person to an appropriate style.

Bottom Lines

> Bad interpersonal relations means bad blood between two people. We almost always want to avoid this.

> Conflict is simply a difference in viewpoint on something. It is inevitable, useful, necessary for creativity. We should encourage it.

> There are tools and techniques to help us avoid bad interpersonal relations and manage conflict. We must learn these approaches, and will ourselves to use them.

Managing Groups:
Building Teamwork

Typical Situation

Meg Howe, the personnel director for a large paper-manufacturing firm, just finished chairing her first session of Task Force Streamline, a group of twelve senior managers appointed by the president to make recommendations for a 10 percent downsizing of the firm.

She was thinking about the group. It was a capable crowd. But three did not want to participate in this effort at all. Another four seemed focused on protecting their departments. And the two brightest were known to be dysfunctional in any kind of group activity. She began thinking of her MBA training. She decided it was time to drag out the books, revisit some of those concepts of group dynamics and team building: "I'm going to need all the help I can get," she thought.

Central Ideas

There are two types of groups encountered in every organization: formal and informal.

- *Formal groups* are prescribed by the organizational blueprint. They include the fixed divisions or departments of the organization. Supplementing this fixed structure we normally find project teams, committees, task forces, and ad hoc groups—all of which are either temporary in nature or have frequently changing memberships.
- *Informal groups* arise spontaneously, often stimulated by friendship or common organizational, professional, or intellectual interests.

Design of the organization's formal groups normally gets the bulk of management attention, as well it should. The first order of business to achieve an effective organization is to decide on a basic structure: the elements needed to do the work and where those elements fit in an overall hierarchy. Supplementing that basic structure are those formal but temporary groups: committees, task forces, projects. These additions to the structure can be critical to optimum functioning. But they should be added with care.

There are three major questions to ask when considering the formation of such groups: What is the purpose of the group? Is a special group needed for this purpose? What is the appropriate size and composition of the group? Periodically, we should review the status of all such groups to determine if they are still needed, and be aggressive in eliminating groups that have outlived their usefulness.

Management usually does a good job on initial design of the structure, but often neglects periodic review. An example, fresh in my mind, makes this point. One of the MBA students at my college wrote her master's thesis on the committee system at her organization, a regional hospital. She had been asked to do this review by the new hospital administrator, so it was also a real-life work project. Her project resulted in the elimination of one third of the existing committees, plus mission and membership changes for all the rest. The need for change was obvious to anyone who looked, but until this project, no one did. Just imagine the multiple implications of this faulty design: misdirected and wasted time, duplication of effort, and poor results. Point: Design with care, and review the design periodically.

Management also needs to be alert to the existence and activities of informal groups. It's amazing how these groups spring up. At the college where I work I've seen the following informal groups rise and fall over the years:

—A book club.

—An investment club with about twelve members.

—A jogging group with six faculty and administrators.

—A brown bag lunch group with a dozen or so faculty, meeting weekly to discuss various issues of interest about the college. Among the topics discussed: mission of the college, size and composition of the core curriculum, faculty pay and benefits, faculty participation in organizational decisionmaking, and promotion policies.

—All tenured faculty decided to hold informal meetings during a several-month period some years ago when the college faced some financial and leadership problems.

Simply because they are not prescribed and somewhat out of sight, informal groups sometimes get ignored by management. Big mistake. Informal groups can generate considerable organizational interest and power, often have a membership that includes key people within the formal organization, and have the capacity to be either dysfunctional or to facilitate the work of the organization. Senior management must keep tuned in to what informal groups are doing. I was a member of that jogging group and you would be amazed (as would management) to hear the issues raised, problems unraveled, and decisions made while puffing up the hills.

Neglecting informal groups can sometimes have severe consequences. An historical case study I use in class makes this point well. Titled "Mass Mutiny Aboard the USS *Constellation*," it is the story of a racial incident occurring on an aircraft carrier in 1972. Black sailors were upset by what they perceived to be a number of unfair policies and practices aboard ship, particularly in the areas of promotion and the administration of discipline. Unable to get a hearing with the ship's captain, they began meeting informally in a remote area of the ship to discuss their grievances. The established Race Relations Council was inadequate to mediate the matter because its membership included no young black sailors (a structural error in forming that group).

The situation escalated to near-mutiny proportions as the captain continued his refusal to recognize or meet with the members of the informal group of black sailors. The navy ultimately had to intervene in the matter, and there was a formal investigation. To the end, the ship's leadership persisted in the view that dealing with the informal group would have been inappropriate. How silly! How disastrous!

The proper management of formal groups begins with proper design, but it doesn't stop there. Monitoring and assessing group functioning is also essential. Results provide one clue to effectiveness, but when bad results arrive, it's too late. A better approach is to keep an eye on group climate and processes, which are usually reliable predictors of ultimate outcomes.

One technique is to examine the group for differences that characterize healthy and unhealthy groups. Some specific characteristics to observe are listed in this chart:

HEALTHY GROUP	UNHEALTHY GROUP
Exhibits democratic leadership	Exhibits autocratic or no leadership
Demonstrates a high degree of permissiveness	Cuts off ideas
Listens attentively to each speaker	Fails to listen carefully
Searches for basic principles, causes	Blames people
Makes group decisions	Permits leader or small clique to make decisions
Takes time to explore and to define problems, objectives, and goals	Permits some members of the group to act before the objective is defined.
Reflects high morale	Reflects low morale

Another approach is to observe the group in actual discussions, watching for specific effective or dysfunctional behaviors. Let's look at some effective and dysfunctional behaviors that typically occur as people work together in groups:

Effective Behavior in Groups
<u>Work or Task Behaviors</u>
   —*Initiating*: Proposing goals or actions; defining problems; suggesting a procedure.
   —*Information giving*: Offering facts; giving an opinion.

—*Checking for meaning*: "Is this what you mean?" "Are you implying that . . . ?"

—*Clarifying*: Interpreting ideas or suggestions; defining terms; clarifying issues before the group.

—*Summarizing*: Pulling together related ideas; restating suggestions; offering a decision or conclusion for the group to consider.

—*Reality testing*: Making a critical analysis of an idea; testing an idea against some data to see if the idea will work.

Group Maintenance Behaviors

—*Harmonizing*: Attempting to reconcile disagreements; reducing tension; getting people to explore differences.

—*Gate keeping*: Helping to keep communication channels open; facilitating the participation of others; suggesting procedures that permit sharing ideas.

—*Consensus testing*: Being friendly, warm, and responsive to others; indicating by facial expression or remarks the acceptance of contributions from others.

—*Compromising:* Offering an alternative that gives others part of what they want while sacrificing part of what you want in the interest of progress or group cohesion.

Dysfunctional Behavior in Groups

—*Displays of aggression*: Deflating status of others; attacking the group for its values; joking in a barbed or semi-concealed way.

—*Blocking*: Disagreeing and opposing beyond "reason"; resisting stubbornly the group's wish for personal reasons; using hidden agenda to thwart group progress.

—*Dominating*: Asserting authority or superiority to ma-
nipulate the group or some of its members; interrupt-
ing contributions of others; controlling by means of
flattery or other forms of patronizing behavior.

—*Playboy behavior*: Displaying, in "playboy" fashion,
one's lack of involvement; "abandoning" the group
while remaining physically with it; seeking recognition in ways not relevant to the group task.

—*Avoidance behavior*: Pursuing special interests not related
to task; staying off the subject to avoid commitment; pre-
venting the group from facing up to controversy.

To sum up—a lot of organizational work is done in groups.
So, to manage your organization, you must be sensitive to
both the design and functioning of the parts (the groups, formal and informal). This is not difficult to do, but it requires
a deliberate effort—you need to look—and the skill to see
problems. The lists provided here (characteristics of healthy/
unhealthy groups and the effective *vs.* dysfunctional behaviors) are a good start, maybe all you really need. Then simply look for opportunities to
check. Sitting in on an occasional
group discussion is helpful, and
it is always good to supplement
personal observations by occasionally and informally asking selected individuals how the group
is working. When you find prob-
lems, you can take action to get things back on track.

◆ **KEY QUOTE** ◆

**"Just putting a bunch of
people in a room together
does not a team make!"**
—Howard and Shelly Gitlow

We ought not leave the subject of managing groups without considering the climate that exists between groups within

the organization. We often do things as managers that pit groups against one another, such as favoring one group, or establishing competitive performance measures. This is always done to promote healthy competition, but it frequently results in bad feelings, we *vs.* they attitudes, and an outcome that has winners and losers. This is dysfunctional to group climate, and it badly serves broader institutional objectives. What we should strive for is a sharing of best practices, and to do that we need a system that emphasizes and rewards cooperation between groups rather than individual group performance.

Situation Revisited

Meg did her homework, reviewed all the material on her shelves about groups and group dynamics. Now she's ready for action.

She first drops in on the president, Mark Irons.

"You gave me a hot potato, boss."

"Don't I know it. Problems?"

"None I can't handle, but I could use your help."

"Anything."

"Well, it's not a big deal, but I'd like you to come to the next meeting. Some on the group are still entertaining the idea that maybe we can avoid downsizing. They actually have not heard you personally speak on this. It will help if you just make clear that the task isn't to find a way around the cut, but to plan how to do it. I'll drop them a note and say you asked for an opportunity to meet with them."

"Consider it done, and thanks for your efforts on this. I know it's a tough job. That's why I gave it to you." He smiled.

Meg's ready for the group at the next meeting. After the president talks and departs, she speaks.

"Before we get to work, I'd like to have you think about something: our work processes. Mark made his point about our job: to give him a downsizing plan. I've been on several committees like this: tough task to do, not much time.

◆ **KEY QUOTE** ◆

"Individual skills are combined so the Group's ability to innovate is something more than the simple sum of its parts."
—**Robert Reich**

"I think it will help us as we proceed to keep an eye on not just our results but on how we are working, together as a group.

"I don't want to make a big deal of it or take a lot of time. But I found two good handouts worth reviewing for a few minutes. The first one [hands it out] contains some characteristics of healthy <u>vs</u>. unhealthy groups. The other one [hands it out] lists a variety of behaviors that typically happen in groups, most functional but also some dysfunctional behaviors.

"I don't think this deserves discussion time here. We've all worked together before. Clearly we are a highly effective bunch. But I would like you to scan these lists and, as we work on this task, consider any actions we might take to improve the process. Might give us an edge."

Meg watches them. They are reading, faces serious. She's thinking: "I've got them. No more arguments about the group's task. Mark settled that. And I'll bet these lists eliminate most dysfunctional behavior. Pretty hard to be aggressive, block, dominate, or avoid participation when you know everyone will immediately recognize it as dysfunctional behavior. I'll still have to keep an eye on things, particularly any informal subgroups that emerge. But I think we can move on now with confidence. Gosh I'm smart!"

Application

❏ Reflect for a moment on your own management practices:

—Do you periodically assess the health and working processes of the formal groups in your organization? How?

—Do you try to stay aware of the status of informal groups in your organization? How?

—Read again the list of effective and dysfunctional behaviors that occur in groups. Do you consciously try to practice the effective behaviors and avoid the dysfunctional behaviors when you participate in group decision making? Do you encourage others to do likewise?

◆   ◆   ◆

❏ Think about the current committees, task forces, and any ad hoc groups in your organization. List any that you feel should be examined in detail for possible elimination or for changes in mission or membership. Order a more detailed examination where appropriate.

◆   ◆   ◆

❏ Does the reward system in your organization promote cooperation or stimulate competition among individuals and groups? Consider whether any changes need to be made in this reward system. If changes are needed, think carefully how they can be implemented.

◆   ◆   ◆

❏ The next time you attend a group meeting, make a point to observe the behaviors going on. Do you find generally effective behaviors? Do you notice any ineffective behaviors? Think carefully about how to guide individuals away from any dysfunctional behaviors.

◆ ◆ ◆

❑ Use the list of healthy and unhealthy group characteristics to assess some group in your organization that is not performing as well as it should. Meet with the group leader to discuss your findings and plot a course of action to improve the group.

Bottom Lines

➤ Ineffective working groups always lead to an ineffective organization.

➤ There are specific techniques for developing healthy groups—those focused on the task and making full use of all group members.

➤ Team building often requires little more than alerting group members to the nature of functional and dysfunctional behavior and having everyone periodically assess how the group is performing. It's not rocket science, but it does require a bit of knowledge and a lot of will.

◆ Module Twelve ◆

Human Resource Management:
Checking the System

Typical Situation

Adam Crow, president of a rapidly expanding retail chain, is perplexed. He thinks, "When we were small, and didn't have all this HRM stuff, things ran well. Now we've got a whole department of specialists looking after the 'people issues' and we are awash with problems. All our old-line and staff leaders are still in place, and they're good. The new HR director—she's doing a lot of new things, but does she know what she's doing? I'd better get myself smarter on this HRM business so I can make an assessment of that area. It's too important to be left to chance."

Central Ideas

No treatment of the topic of managing others would be complete without addressing the human resource management (HRM) system of the organization. A senior manager could have excellent personal skills in motivation, leadership, negotiation, influence, power, interpersonal relations, conflict management, and the management of groups—and still do a poor job of managing others because of a faulty HRM system.

I have found that most executives are quite good at seeing weak spots in the HRM system, if they look. But often they don't look. The main obstacle to their looking seems to be the lack of a good framework or lens. HRM systems have many parts, so a comprehensive model can help you to assess them. My purpose here is to describe such a model, provide some thoughts on its use, and direct your attention to its application.

There are four main functions involved in the HRM task: attracting good people to the organization, developing their skills, motivating them to good performance, and keeping them committed to the organization.

A descriptive model of the HRM system is provided on the next page. Study it briefly now. It is an excellent tool to assess your system. Though the model is fairly self-explanatory, let me offer a few thoughts that should assist you in understanding and applying it.

● *Strategic human resource planning* involves determining the organization's human resource needs, strategies, and philosophies. It must be done with the organization's overall strategy in mind. Thus it demands the attention of top management.

● *The HRM system has a lot of interrelated parts*. Every manager and supervisor in the organization plays a part in its administration. Without careful supervision, implementation problems are likely to occur. Consequently, senior managers must periodically assess the system.

● *Recruiting, selection, and job assignment* are critical activities. The care with which they are done sends impor-

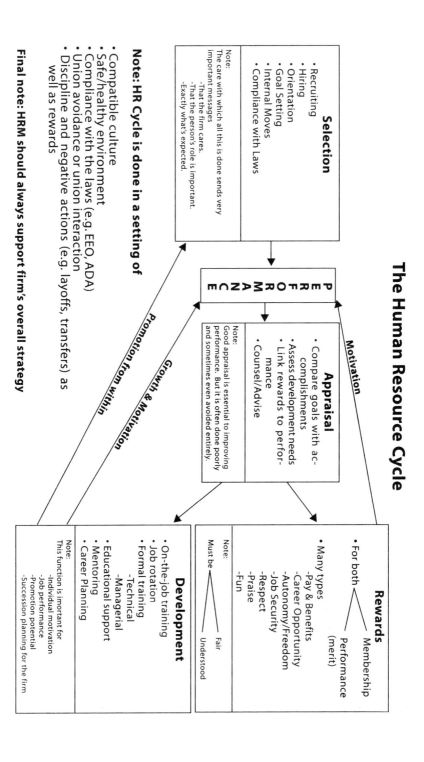

tant messages: that the firm cares, that the individual's role is important, and that the firm expects certain results from each individual. Recruiting, hiring, orientation, and individual goal setting are fairly mechanical processes and are done on many levels. But the role of top management is critical. The tasks of the executive are to establish an overall organizational climate that attracts good people, and to ensure through continuous evaluation that the HRM process is working. This takes both knowledge of HRM and attention to the organization's HRM system.

● *Performance appraisal* is handled badly in most organizations. Managers typically hate to do it. It takes a lot of time to do correctly, and a good performance appraisal involves addressing performance shortcomings, which can be uncomfortable. To be done right it must be done often, verbally, and informally—not just once a year with the company's evaluation form. There's more to it than simply providing a score sheet comparing goals with accomplishments. The appraisal system must also assess development needs, educate subordinates on the linkage between rewards and performance, and provide appropriate advice and follow-up assistance. The process is important to the organization's people and thus to the organization's performance. Getting it done well requires continuous top management oversight. However, it is also an area where senior executives have an opportunity to teach and lead by example as they appraise the performance of those reporting directly to them.

● Some of the major components of the *reward system* are shown in the model. Typically we don't think creatively enough about rewards. A lot of attention is given to pay and benefits; less thought is given to other types of rewards. It is important to look at four things relative to the reward system: Is it fair, does it reward for performance (merit) as well as for membership, does it make use of a sufficiently wide range of rewards and incentives, and is it understood by everyone in the organization?

● *Development* is another area where we often operate with a half-full tool bag. The list of development activities in the model must be part of every HRM system. Development is important to individual growth and motivation, and it's essential to the organization's capacity to promote from within.

In any overall assessment of the HRM system we must look at the system as a totality. A weakness in one part of the system can have an impact elsewhere. An inadequate reward system can handicap recruiting; bad performance appraisals miss training needs and development opportunities; training-and-development shortcomings prevent promotion from within. The list of problems is endless.

Thus, all parts of the model must be examined, first in isolation, then for interconnections with the other parts. And this must be done with an eye to such related issues as health and safety, compliance with the law, union implications, any requirements for discipline or negative actions (e.g., layoffs, transfers), and the overall culture of the organization.

It is often said, quite rightly, that your people are your most important asset. Getting and keeping good people is the most important job of management. Taking your eye off the system spells trouble. Let me cite a personal example.

I once commanded an army artillery group of about 4,000 soldiers—four battalions of three batteries each. Each battery had five officers, young lieutenants. The military efficiency reports (ER's) were critical to promotion. In those days one negative sentence or the suggestion of a weakness could stop a promotion cold. The performance evaluation system in my group was such that the person rating these lieutenants was their battery commander (typically another lieutenant, perhaps a year more senior). The report was then endorsed at the battalion level and sent to the Department of the Army (DA).

Two months into my command tour I wasn't concerned about this process. I wasn't going around looking for problems. I had enough biting me. But a Lieutenant Cox came to see me one day with his ER in hand. I knew him and thought highly of him. The report, as written, would have killed his career and he was smart enough to know it. I still recall the awkward way he approached me. He didn't feel he knew me very well, didn't know how I'd react, wasn't even sure I'd see his problem as serious.

The encounter went like this:

"Sir, I'd like you to take a look at this report—tell me what you think."

"You're a dead man, with this in your file."

"That's what I thought. What can be done?"

"I don't know. You get along well with the battery commander?"

"Yes, at least I thought so. Still do. He handed me this report sort of routinely. I think he sees it as an overall favorable report on a young guy who still has much to learn."

"Thanks for coming in. You did the right thing. I'll look into it, and get back to you."

He left. I called the battery commander, a very serious and capable guy.

"Lieutenant Cox came to see me today."

"Really, what about?"

"His ER."

"What's the problem?"

"Don't know yet. What do you think of him—his performance, future promotion potential?"

"He's doing well. Another year's experience and he'll be able to take my job."

To make a long story short, I recognized I had a big problem on my hands: Young commanders who did not know the system, killing off good subordinates unintentionally. Fortunately, Lieutenant Cox's report had not gone to the DA. It was rewritten appropriately. I immediately directed that all ER's would cross my desk on the way to the DA, a stopgap measure to see no one else got hurt while we were correcting the system. This was followed by a groupwide education program on the army efficiency report system and the characteristics of good and bad reports.

> ◆ **KEY QUOTE** ◆
>
> **"The systems that fail are those that rely on the permanency of human nature, and not on its growth and development."**
> **—Oscar Wilde**

I was always grateful to that lieutenant for coming to see me. He called my attention to a very serious problem. Without my intervention, think what might have happened: marginal reports on lots of good people hurting both the morale of the individuals and resulting ultimately in the loss of capable people to the army.

Also, through our actions we were able to educate a lot of people who would carry that knowledge and philosophy into other organizations. A lot of good was done. But the message must not be lost: HRM systems need to be monitored carefully, by the boss.

Situation Revisited

Adam contacted a friend who taught management at a local university. He was told that the best way to get really smart about HRM was to read a good textbook on the subject. His friend said: "I wouldn't suggest a textbook in most areas of management, but HRM is different. It's got very distinct pieces: recruiting, compensation, performance appraisal, etc. A textbook will give you a lot of depth in each area. You can read first those parts that most concern you and pick up the others later."

On the way home Adam picked up an HRM textbook. Over the weekend he read the introductory chapters for an overview of the field, then concentrated on the chapter on compensation. Two recommendations on his desk from his new HR director involved developing a merit pay system and offering employees more flexible benefits packages.

Adam thought: "I'll start with these two compensation proposals. I'll drop her [HR director] a note saying I'd like to meet to discuss these two proposals in detail before acting on them. This discussion will give me a feel for how she thinks. It will also serve notice on her that I am a hands-on guy who intends to be involved in major issues in her area. And, by confining this discussion to compensation, I think she'll see me as reasonably competent—which I will be in all areas once I finish with this book."

Application

❏ Reflect for a moment on your own management practices:

—When was the last time you personally participated

in a comprehensive assessment of your HRM system?

—Do you personally set a good example in conducting performance appraisals?

—Do you habitually think in terms of the full range of rewards and development approaches listed in the model?

—Do you consciously try to maintain an organizational culture and climate that facilitates attracting and retaining good people?

◆　◆　◆

❏ Give a copy of the model to your organization's HR director. Ask that a briefing be prepared for you covering each major area.

◆　◆　◆

❏ Before listening to the briefing, make your own crude assessment of each of these areas. Try to identify weak spots in your system and develop questions to ask during the briefing. Use the ideas discussed in this section to help you identify weak areas and appropriate questions.

◆　◆　◆

❏ Invite key members of your staff to attend the briefing. Begin with emphasizing how important this area is and how all managers get involved in the various functions. Ask everyone to put on their thinking caps.

Bottom Lines

➢ A faulty HRM system can foul up an organization, in spite of otherwise good leadership and management practices.

➤ Recruiting, selection, orientation, performance appraisal, training, development, reward systems: Any of these things can throw a monkey wrench into the operation. They cannot be left totally in the hands of HR specialists.

➤ Senior managers need enough knowledge of HRM to kick the tires, check the system, see to it that the system is sound and that it supports the overall thrust of the organization.

➤ Knowledge in this area doesn't always come simply from good management instincts. HRM is a highly specialized field. Study is required. An HRM textbook is your best resource.

Part Three

Managing Organizations

A Systems Approach To Management:
Seeing the Parts—and the Whole

Typical Situation

Caroline Thompson, manager of a large ski resort in Colorado, is doing some homework. She has hired a consultant to perform an assessment of the resort. He begins tomorrow by interviewing her, and he has asked her to prepare a concise overview of the organization: "A description of the organization, and your own personal assessment of the situation."

Pen poised, Caroline wonders: "Where do I start? How can I get my arms around this thing? Why is he asking me? If I could do this I wouldn't need a consultant."

Central Ideas

It is essential for the executive to think of the organization as a total system. Lower levels of management may have the luxury of a piecemeal approach, but not senior management.

The necessary tool is a comprehensive model to use as a lens to view the organization. This avoids missing important parts or issues. I've examined various systems models. The best I've found (and it is truly outstanding) is the model offered by Kast and Rosenzweig in their text *Organization and Management: A Systems and Contingency Approach.*

The model, shown below, depicts the organization as five interrelated subsystems: goals and values, technology, structure, psychosocial, and management—separated by a boundary from the external environment. The external environment consists of everything outside the organization's boundary that impacts the organization: individuals, other organizations, or factors like the economy and the state of technology.

It's called an open systems model because the boundaries can and must be penetrated. The organization must be able to exchange information and resources with its environment. Management, in this model, can be considered the force that glues the other subsystems together and links the organization to the external world.

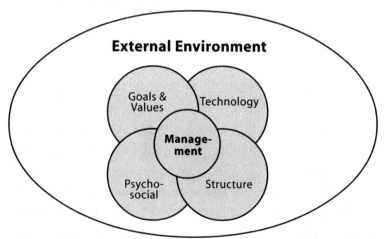

Source: *Organization and Management: A Systems and Contingency Approach* by Fremont E. Kast and James E. Rosenzweig. New York: McGraw-Hill, 1985. Used with permission.

The following story illustrates how the model works. Some years ago I was flying across the country. The passenger next to me was a manager in a government research laboratory. He told me the laboratory's management had gone steadily downhill following the hiring of a new laboratory director.

My seatmate said: "We once had a great lab. The director was a good administrator. Technical people were organized into four major divisions. I headed one. There were regular meetings. There was a sense of order about the place. Then this new director was hired, a super mind, a near-Nobel Prize winner. He started bringing in a lot of people from the outside, abolished the divisional structure, and now has sixteen scientists reporting directly to him. He never holds meetings, spends most of his time on his own research, and doesn't know what's going on in the lab."

My seatmate and I started to think about his laboratory using the systems model. What we found amazed us both, and convinced us that this new lab director was a pretty shrewd guy. Apparently the Department of Energy (DOE) (in the external environment of the lab) had been continually sending a goals-and-values message across the boundaries of the laboratory, telling it to get more innovative. No one paid attention.

The DOE got tired of waiting and decided to hire the new lab director. In the terms of the model, the DOE imported new technology (a highly qualified scientist) across the organization's boundaries from the external environment. To get this person they had to make him lab director. To get the innovation he wanted, the new director had to bring in people that he knew, again importing technology from the environment. Finally, to get these bright people he had to change the structure, flattening it so these new scientists would report directly to him. This upset the psychosocial subsystem. (My seatmate was angry, as were others who had suffered status change.)

◆ **KEY QUOTE** ◆

"Systems thinking shows us that there is no outside; that you and the cause of your problems are part of a single system."
—Peter Senge

This new lab director had viewed the organization as a total system. He knew that making changes in one subsystem impacted the others, and he knew he had to exchange resources with the external environment to meet his innovation goals. He was not inept, as my seatmate had thought. He had traded control for the innovation demanded by the DOE, a key force in the lab's external environment. This story illustrates a number of things about the workings of the model:

- Penetrable boundaries are essential to hear messages and obtain resources from the outside world.
- Goals and values are not constants and not always obvious. Profit, service, and organizational survival are three fairly common goals. But in this laboratory's case, innovation became a key goal.
- Technology obviously includes equipment or facilities. But it is more than that. It includes anything that makes the organization work smarter. In this case it was new scientific talent.
- When a change is made to one subsystem, the other subsystems normally change in response. The pressure of new goals and values caused technology

changes at the lab which resulted in changes in the management, structural and psychosocial subsystems.

Situation Revisited

Caroline calls in Amy Fry. Amy's one of the ski instructors, a good friend, and a recent MBA grad. Caroline explains her dilemma. Amy sketches out the systems model and explains how to use it. The conversation went like this:

"How will this model help?" asked Caroline.

"It lets you see all the parts, issues, aspects of the organization. And it's a good way to structure your presentation, organize it according to the subsystems."

"Sounds good, but I'm not sure I can do it."

"Let me get you started. Let's look at the technology subsystem. What do you see?"

"Our new computer system."

"OK, that's part of it. But you have so much more here by way of technology. Remember, you have the ski slopes. The rental equipment, ski lifts, snowmaking machines, and instructors are all part of the resort's technology. And you have a hotel and three restaurants which not only require an expanded management structure, but have key elements of technology."

"Like what?"

"Well, for starters, cooks and all kinds of maintenance and service personnel. Everything that helps the resort to run efficiently is part of your technology."

"I think I get the message. I'll make a stab at all the subsystems and check back with you. Maybe you'll see some things I don't."

"Fine, I'll be around all day."

Caroline starts to work. "Let's see," she thinks, "goals and values: safe slopes, enough snow, competent instruction, comfortable rooms, good food. I think I'm going to be good at this."

Application

❏ The best way to appreciate the power of the systems model is to use it. So, try this simple experiment. Think about two different kinds of prisons:

—A prison to incarcerate hardened criminals.
—A prison to rehabilitate prisoners and return them to society.

Your simple gut reaction would tell you some of the differences. But try using the systems model for your analysis. Under each subsystem (goals and values, technology, structure, etc.), list the relevant characteristics of each prison. For example, the first prison would be staffed with lots of tough guards, the second with counselors and teachers and a more modest security element.

◆ ◆ ◆

❏ If you liked that exercise, try another. Compare the differences between two kinds of kid's baseball teams:

—Little League baseball, the very organized teams now in every community.
—Sandlot baseball, games played by a bunch of kids who meet spontaneously on a vacant lot in the neighborhood.

◆ ◆ ◆

❏ Think now about your own practices. When confronted with organizational problems, do you typically take a total systems view? What model or conceptual framework have you been using as a lens? Is your model as comprehensive as the Kast and Rosenzweig model? If not, consider using this model until you find a better one (and if you do, send me a copy, please).

◆   ◆   ◆

❏ Think now about your own organization. Use the Kast and Rosenzweig systems model to describe and critique your organization. Then hold a meeting of key people, and, using your personal analysis of the organization as a starting point, have the group contribute to the development of a more detailed analysis.

Bottom Lines

➤ Managers must be capable of making a preliminary assessment of their organizations.

➤ There's nothing wrong with hiring a consultant to do an in-depth analysis, to check and extend one's own thinking. But a manager's personal analysis is useful as a guide for the consultant and as a rough check on the consultant's findings.

➤ The key to any analysis is a comprehensive lens, a systems model that focuses attention on all the important factors and features of the organization. This chapter provides one such a model.

Analysis of the External Environment:
Tackling the Outside World

Typical Situation

Tim Bacon, owner and chief executive of a book publishing firm, is concerned. He had arranged this three-day management retreat for his senior managers, to develop a set of short- and long-term initiatives for the organization. Today, the first day, the group attempted to describe the present and future external environment of the organization: the outside forces, factors, and players that could impact the firm. They'd hired a pretty skilled consultant who had worked them hard at the task. Lots of ideas from everyone.

But as the session broke up Tim thought, "This was useful, but too fragmented. How will we ever bring closure to it? How can I tell when we've found all the important players or factors? And what do we do about those we find?"

Central Ideas

Every system can be thought of as a subsystem of some

larger environment. From the organization's viewpoint, its external environment is everything beyond its boundaries that affects operations: factors, conditions, individuals, and other organizations.

The external environment is important for two reasons. First, the toughest management problems today don't involve managing single organizations, but making multiple organizational systems work together. Second, to solve the most demanding organizational problems and capitalize on important new opportunities, we must normally look to the external environment for information and resources.

A proactive approach to the analysis of the external environment is essential in complex and rapidly changing environments. An internally oriented organization is not likely to survive. Even a general awareness of the environment may not be sufficient. What is required is a continuous review of the external environment using a comprehensive, systematic, and proactive approach. We must see what is critical in the environment and act in a timely way—before being forced to react to unexpected challenges. It can be done. I'll suggest a system for doing it and let you try your hand at applying it.

A system or framework for analyzing the external environment is provided by the model in this section (page 153). It suggests a set of environmental categories to assist in identifying the critical players or factors in the environment. However, simply knowing what's in the environment is not enough. Action is the goal. So the model provides a process to determine any required action. Look again at the model. Note that for each player or factor in the environment you must identify three things:

- The type of impact on the organization.
- The status of the relationship.
- The proposed action.

The power of this system stems from two features. First, it provides a mechanism to identify all of the relevant players or factors. Second, it forces us to focus on actions relative to each player or factor.

Note that the environment is divided into two types: general and specific. The general environment is applicable to all organizations and is comprised of four categories: technology, the economy, social values, and institutions. The specific environment is only applicable to one organization and is comprised of five categories: clients, suppliers, advisors, controllers, and adversaries.

Two examples from my world should help you understand the model as you apply it to your organization. (After reading each example, note how it is entered into the model.)

1. An *institution* and also a *controller* in the environment of my college is the Middle States Accreditation Team. This team visits the college for a week every ten years. Its impact is important to us. An unfavorable

---

♦ KEY QUOTE ♦

"Competition will bite you if you keep running ... stand still, it will swallow you."

—Semon Emil Knudsen

review could shut down the college. The status of our relationship with this team has always been excellent. For its last visit we began preparations eighteen months in advance. To reinforce an already good relationship, our first proposed action was to invite them to the college eighteen months before the scheduled evaluation, to get their views on the best approach to prepare for their formal visit. That got us off to a good start. And our subsequent actions to maintain close contact with this team led to valuable advice throughout our preparation and resulted in a very favorable evaluation.

2. In the *specific environment* we have a set of advisors for many of our academic departments. In the case of my department, we have the Business Advisory Committee, a group of business executives and educators who meet with us once a year and provide advice on our academic programs. Its role is important to us. It is particularly valuable to us as a validation group for ideas we'd like to try.

Our relationship with this group has always been excellent. But during the years I chaired the department, I found that two things were very important to maintaining that relationship. First, group members wanted to be sure that their views got heard beyond the department level. They wanted to be heard by the president.

◆ **Key Quote** ◆

"Be ever fearful of trouble when all seems fair and clear, for the easy is soon made grievous by the swift-transforming sphere."
—Nasir-C-Khusran (c. 1004-1061)

Second, they wanted to see action taken on their recommendations. To satisfy their wishes I always prepared a memorandum to the president identifying all their recommenda-

A SYSTEM FOR ANALYSIS OF THE EXTERNAL ENVIRONMENT

	Environmental Categories	Players or Factors by Category	Type Impact on the Organization by Players or Factors	Status of Relationship	Proposed Action
General Environment	Social Values				
	The Economy				
	Technology				
	Institutions	Middle states accreditation team	They evaluate college and can shut you down	Excellent/Helpful	Maintain contact with them for advice during preparation for their visit
Specific Environment	Clients (receivers of services)				
	Suppliers (provide resources)				
	Advisors (assist in use of resources)	Business Advisory Committee	They can validate your ideas and suggest new ideas for the business program	Very helpful but want their ideas to receive consideration by top management	Provide their recommendations to the president in writing and send them a copy of that memo and let them know what action was taken
	Controllers (set rules, sanction)				
	Adversaries (rivals; enemies)				

tions. I then sent all members a copy soon after the meeting.

Further, at the start of each annual meeting, I provided them a summary of their previous recommendations with the actions that had been taken. Also, I made a point of explaining the reasons for any lack of action.

Analysis of the external environment is demanding work. Since we are always interested in predicting the future environment, it also calls for a high order of creativity. It is not something for the executive to do alone. The entire senior management team must be involved, supported by the necessary internal staff and often by external consultants.

Situation Revisited

As the meeting ended, Tim approached the consultant, Doris Hardy. She smiled brightly and asked: "How do you think it went, Tim?"

Tim, not too convincingly: "Pretty good, so far . . . say, can we talk a bit after the dinner tonight? I've got some concerns."

Doris: "Sure, right after dinner, see you then."

Dinner's over. Tim and Doris grab the last of the coffee, pick a back table and begin discussing the retreat. Doris starts: "You're not happy with today?"

"No, that's not it. The day went well. We got a lot of stuff on the table."

"But . . ."

"Well, our ideas seem scattered. My hope for this retreat was that we'd identify all the important environmental factors and nail down the actions we need to take."

"We will. Come with me."

Doris took Tim into the meeting room where she had posted big charts: the framework for analysis discussed here. They were partly filled out with all the things discussed at the day's meeting. She described the model, then added, "I wanted the initial discussion to be unrestricted to get all the creativity possible from the group. Tomorrow I'll force them to flesh out the model. That will bring more order to the process and ensure comprehensiveness. OK?"

"Great. I love it. I know why I hired you!"

Application

❑ Think for a moment about your present organization and the management practices there (yours and others).

— How is the organization structured to analyze the external environment? Who is responsible? Who participates? When is it done?

— When was the last time you were intimately involved in the process? Did you think the process was sound? Did you take action if you did not consider the process sound?

— How would you rate your personal grasp of the elements of your organization's external environment? Have you targeted specific environmental elements for action?

◆ ◆ ◆

❑ Using the framework provided here, perform your own personal analysis of the external environment of your organization.

(You'll need to increase the size of the model on page 153 to chart or blackboard size.)

◆ ◆ ◆

❑ Call on several smart internal people to help you refine your analysis.

❑ Arrange a meeting of the senior management team to review the analysis. Send out your own analysis well before the meeting, asking each participant to come prepared to improve it.

◆   ◆   ◆

❑ At the meeting have the team recommend:

—The actions needed relative to each identified player or factor in the environment.

—The actions needed to ensure that the organization follows up to continuously maintain a comprehensive assessment of its external environment.

Bottom Lines

➤ An internally oriented organization is not likely to survive today.

➤ The future of most complex organizations is profoundly influenced by forces, factors, and players external to the organization.

➤ What's needed is a continuous and systematic approach to finding all the important elements in this external environment, and determining the necessary action to deal with each element.

➤ The key to a thorough analysis is a comprehensive framework, a model providing categories to assist in finding all the important elements, and proposing appropriate action relative to each. This chapter provides such a framework. Try it!

◆ Module Fifteen ◆

Organizational Culture: Answering—What Are We Like? How Should We Be?

Typical Situation

Craig Edwards, owner of a rapidly growing chain of popular bagel restaurants, is flying to California to look for new sites. On his lap are three different business publications, each with articles citing the importance of a firm's culture. He's heard it all before, but never stopped to really think about it. Now he is. He thinks, "There's obviously something to this, something I ought to understand and examine in our business. It can't hurt and it might help. But, how do I go about it? I don't even know how to intelligently think about corporate cultures."

Central Ideas

Organizational culture is a system of values and beliefs that characterizes the organization and guides the behavior of its members. Culture is important. It deserves the attention of senior management.

Two landmark studies conducted in the 1980s confirm the importance of culture to an organization's performance.

- The Deal and Kennedy study of eighty companies reported in their book, *Corporate Cultures: The Rites and Rituals of Corporate Life.*
- The Peters and Waterman study of sixty-two companies published in their book, *In Search of Excellence: Lessons From American's Best Run Companies.*

Both studies found a strong correlation between strong corporate cultures and organizational achievement. Peters and Waterman reported that "without exception, the dominance and coherence of culture proved to be an essential quality of the excellent companies." Numerous subsequent studies emphasized the same point.

◆ **KEY QUOTE** ◆

"A vision without a task is but a dream, a task without a vision is drudgery, a vision and a task is the hope of the world."
—1730, in a Church in Sussex, England

Deal and Kennedy did the best job of defining culture. You rarely find a management text written in the past dozen years that does not use their description of culture. I wouldn't attempt to improve on it. They identify five elements of any organizational culture.

1. *The Business Environment*, defined by the core activity of the business (manufacturing, selling services, research). This is the greatest force in shaping an organization's culture.
2. *Values*, the organization's basic beliefs about the right

way to do things. Values define for employees how they must act in the organization to succeed.

3. *Heroes*, the people (past and present) who display the core values and personify the culture. Heroes are role models for employees.

4. *Rites and Rituals*, the routines of day-to-day life in the company plus events that honor the heroes and celebrate success. These reinforce company values and underline the kind of behavior expected.

5. *Cultural Network*, the system of information, relationships and communication that exists within the organization. It, too, spreads the corporate values.

The culture impacts management practices within the organization:

—Is leadership directive or participative?

—Is decision making centralized or decentralized?

—Does communication flow from the top down, or in every direction?

—Does management exercise high control or do individuals exercise a high degree of self-control?

—Is willing compliance the key to individual success, or is creativity valued and rewarded?

The culture not only influences how people act, it is a determining factor in who chooses to join the organization, how they perform once hired, and whether they like it enough to stay—all vital concerns of senior management.

We see the elements of culture in every organization. In combat units of the military, bravery is a high value, and much ritual surrounds the awarding of medals for heroism in battle. Those honored typically wear their decorations routinely. Their deeds follow them through official records and informally through the cultural network.

In colleges, both good teaching and academic scholarship are valued. Promotion of faculty to senior rank requires doing both well. Publication of a book is cause for campuswide celebration honoring the author.

A manufacturing firm where I've consulted places its highest value on output: pounds of product produced per unit time. Much ritual surrounds the annual award to the best plant. Important contributors are recognized as well. Heroes are made by consecutive wins.

No one culture is "best" for all organizations. Culture is highly situational. And the right culture does not find the organization—the organization must find its own culture and nurture it. Doing so doesn't take genius, but it does take skill and effort—to assess, fine tune, and maintain the culture. The first step is to examine the culture, and the Dean and Kennedy construct is a good lens to use. It helps you see the "what is" of the culture. Then comes the hard work: assessing its effectiveness and changing it as necessary. The application section of this chapter will suggest approaches to the assessment process. Chapter 18 (Managing Change) can help if you find change is necessary.

One final point: Don't be surprised if you find many cultures existing simultaneously in your organization. A few years ago a colleague of mine and I were invited to write a journal article on the culture of the military. We found quite different cultures within the army: troop units in combat, troop units in training, Pentagon staffs, military service schools—all had different values, types of heroes, rituals, and cultural networks. And it's no great leap to see significant differences in the culture in other military services. For example, the air

force typically operates more informally than the navy. And the culture aboard a submarine is quite different than that on an aircraft carrier. The point: Cultures can differ greatly even within the same organization. But one fact remains— good cultures are those that work!

Situation Revisited

Alone in a small California city, and still troubled by the culture question, Craig seeks out a good bookstore, a local Barnes & Noble where Starbucks provides food for mind and body. Two hours later, having browsed through a stack of books, he heads for his hotel, ready for action.

It's 9:00 p.m. in California, midnight at his headquarters in Baltimore. Craig calls his partner Len Shultz: "What are you doing?"

"I was sleeping. It's midnight you know."

"Yeah, wanted to get your attention."

"About what?"

"Organization culture."

"You been drinking?"

"Coffee only. But I've been thinking and reading."

"I'm happy for you. But is there a message for me in this, Craig?"

"Definitely. I'll prove my point when I see you. But I've become convinced that finding the right culture is important. Companies with strong cultures do better."

"I've heard this, and I guess I agree, but why this call?"

"I don't think we have ever consciously looked at our culture. My conclusion after digging through several books on the subject is that an assessment will pay off for us. I don't think we're completely on target."

"What can I do, Craig? It's midnight."

"Sorry about that. But tomorrow I'd like you to call that friend of yours who heads the Johns Hopkins Management Program. Get us a good name, someone with a solid background in organizational culture and also some process skills, someone who can advise and help us in an assessment. Set up a meeting for us with this person for next week. Then we'll figure out what to do next."

"Good night, Craig."

"Sorry ... thanks."

Application

❑ Think back through your whole career experience for a moment.

—Identify the organization in your career history that had what you consider the strongest culture.

—What was the business environment (e.g., manufacturing, selling services, doing research)?

—What were the top three values of the organization?

—Name several "heroes" (individuals who personified the culture).

—Identify two important rites or rituals of that organization. What impact did they have on you? Did they affect your behavior?

—Identify two significant people in the cultural network—individuals who spread the word on the organization's values.

◆   ◆   ◆

❑ Arrange a meeting of several trusted colleagues for the purpose of assessing the nature and strength of your organization's culture. Send them a copy of the central ideas in this section. Ask them to come to the meeting with their ideas on the various elements of culture as they apply to your organization.

◆   ◆   ◆

❑ At the meeting try to develop an initial assessment by brainstorming ideas. What are the organization's values, rites and rituals? Who are the most respected heroes? Who are the prime movers in the cultural network?

◆   ◆   ◆

❑ Decide whether the group considers the culture weak or strong. Try to identify some steps to improve it. If you can't see how to improve it, try to decide on an approach to getting help with the task.

Bottom Lines

➤ An organization's culture is the way it does things, the way its members behave. The foundation of the culture is the organization's values and its approach to institutionalizing those values.

➤ Many studies have found a strong relationship between the performance of an organization and the nature and strength of its culture. This is understandable because the culture influences who is attracted to the organization, who gets hired, how they perform once hired, and whether they stay.

➤ Designing, assessing, and managing the culture are important functions of senior-level leadership. Strong cultures will not happen by accident.

Organization Assessment: Finding What's Going Right— And Wrong

Typical Situation

Beth Haynes, vice president of marketing for a defense contractor, was relaxing on the airplane. But she was thinking. The professor from MIT sitting next to her, Jerry Schmidt, had made her think. He was a consultant to NASA, and during dinner they had talked about the causes of NASA's *Challenger* disaster. Something the professor said really struck home:"They focused on past success as a measure of their organizational effectiveness. Big mistake. The current health of work processes, like planning and decision-making processes, is the true measure of effectiveness. And keeping track of such processes calls for continuous assessment. NASA did not do it."

"Neither do we," thought Beth. "I wonder how we can get started."

Central Ideas

In assessing our organizations, we often lean heavily on the record: how the organization has performed in the past.

That's worth looking at certainly. It's our score sheet, and a bad score is a clue that something is wrong. But there's a problem with this approach. A good past record is not always an accurate predictor of the future, and contemplating a successful past can lead to false complacency.

Assuming the organization is in the right business, the best predictor of future performance is the current health of its working processes. Most managers I've talked to agree with that idea, but they lack techniques for assessing the processes. Traditional assessment approaches all have major limitations. The suggestion box approach generates ideas, but they are normally negative ideas and one never knows how many people share those same thoughts. Surveys can be helpful, but surveys limit what people can say to the questions asked. I will propose here a method for fully focusing the brain power of the organization on the assessment task.

The general method is called the Nominal Group Technique. I'm going to first outline an adaptation of this technique developed by a former teacher of mine, Neely Gardner of the University of Southern California. Then I'll discuss an excursion from Neely's approach which I developed and have used over and over again in consulting assignments, always with success.

Neely was famous for his approach. It can be used to assess the processes of the organization, or the status of a specific project, or test organizational opinion of a new idea or policy. It is simple and powerful. You get everyone's opinion of what is good and bad, and you find the number of people who agree or disagree on every opinion offered. You really do find the truth.

Let's assume you want to do an overall assessment of the

health of the working processes in your organization. The steps are as follows:

- Assemble for a day or two all the people you would like to participate in the assessment. You need at least ten people to fully capitalize on this method. Over twenty-five becomes cumbersome. And, or course, you must have the right people assembled: Those who know the organization and are responsible for its functioning. Explain to the group this whole sequence of steps in advance. Assure everyone that all responses will be completely anonymous, and ask each person to respect the privacy of others while participating.
- Give each person three blank cards, each of a different color, say green, red, and yellow.
- Ask them to write on the green card that feature of the organization's working processes that they most like, that they would not change under any circumstances (e.g., "I like the uniformly high-quality people on our management team").
- Ask them to write on the red card the thing they most dislike about the working processes and would stop if they could (e.g., "Daily staff meetings; we don't need to meet every day").
- Ask them to write on the yellow card their best constructive suggestion for improving the working processes (e.g., "Schedule two planning retreats each year instead of one").
- Assemble all the cards and have all the ideas converted to simple statements that can be voted on by all participants. You might want to have three subgroups develop the three lists from the information

on the cards. Or you might have a consultant do this while the group takes a break.

- Distribute the three lists of statements and have each individual anonymously vote on each item using the following scale:

  5 = strongly agree
  4 = agree
  3 = neutral
  2 = disagree
  1 = strongly disagree
  0 = don't know enough to vote

- Collect the voting sheets and tabulate the data (again by subgroups or by a consultant). Be sure to show the distribution of responses (i.e., the strength of agreement) on each statement. There might be a temptation to average the numbers, but this could produce a very false conclusion. For example, if the respondents were evenly split with strong feelings (half strongly agreeing and half strongly disagreeing), averaging would indicate neutrality, which clearly would be misleading. So show the full distribution on each item.

Consider what information you have at this point. You have the best ideas of what to keep doing, what to stop doing, and what to change. You have it from each participant. And you have the reaction of the entire group to each item submitted. Powerful stuff!

There are many ways to proceed from this point. One is to distribute the data and begin to brainstorm appropriate actions. I prefer to break into small subgroups, ask each subgroup to develop proposed actions relative to a subset of the statements, and have all participants react to subgroup briefings of their proposed actions. This uses the full brainpower of the participants.

I have used Neely's method dozens of times in facilitating annual retreats for organizations. It always works well. The only problem I've noted is a time issue. Doing all the list making, voting, and data tabulation takes time which could be better spent discussing problems and developing action plans. So, in the past few years I've experimented with a slight excursion. I get all the data through mailings prior to the meeting.

It's simple to do. I write each person well before the meeting, explain the method, and ask for their input (practices they like and dislike, plus suggested changes). Usually I ask for two or three items in each category. I tell them not to sign their input sheets, and I include a self-addressed envelope. When I get the input, I make up the lists of statements to vote on, send them back to everyone, get the responses back in the mail, and assemble the data—all before the actual meeting. At the meeting there is typically little argument about what needs to be done—the issue is how. Action planning can start immediately, much work gets done, and individuals leave with the feeling of a very productive session.

> ◆ **KEY QUOTE** ◆
>
> **"Generally, management of many is the same as management of few. It is a matter of organization."**
> **—Sun-Tzu**

In describing this method I have concentrated on its usefulness in addressing and improving the working processes of the organization. It can be equally effective in assessing organizational goals or specific programs or policies. The question is framed the same: what do you like, dislike, and suggest changing regarding the specific goal, program, or policy?

Situation Revisited

Beth and Jerry are waiting to pick up their bags. Beth decides it's now or never. She needs help.

"Jerry, I need your advice."

"On assessment?"

"Yes, could you spare me a half hour? Buy you a beer."

"Sure, I'm in no big hurry."

Beth explains her marketing organization, and her conviction that it badly needs assessment of its processes. Jerry listens with interest.

"So, Jerry, what do you think?"

"Assessment is probably in order if you've never done it. A tune-up always helps."

"How do I get it done?"

"Nominal Group Technique is a powerful method. Always works for me."

"Can you help? Can you facilitate it?"

"Not personally, Beth. I'm totally tied up for the next few months. But I have a good article explaining the method. I'll send it to you. And there's a Ph.D. candidate at MIT who has been doing some very successful meeting facilitation work as part of his dissertation. He could do the job."

"Sounds interesting. Look, send me the article. I'll try to get our people to agree to a retreat for this. Then I'll contact you and you can put me in touch with this facilitator."

"Sure thing, I'll send it to you next week."

Beth, in the hot tub at the hotel, is relaxed but thinking: "We need this. Since I took the job two years ago we've been so busy doing things we have not stopped for a minute to check our working processes. This is bound to help—a tune up. I may have a little trouble selling it to a few of the folks, but I'm determined to do it. I'll start with a light memo on my conversation with Jerry, circulate his article. We'll get there."

Application

❏ Without any outside assistance, reflect on the state of health of the working processes of your organization.

> —List what you consider to be the five best things about the processes.
> —List what you consider to be the five worst things about the processes.
> —List your five best constructive suggestions to improve the processes.

◆   ◆   ◆

❏ If you can find five items in each category, you can bet your management team can find a lot more. So, I suggest you proceed as follows, trying the method described here.

> —Pick a subset of five individuals from the management team simply to test the method. Pick five respected opinion formers.
> —Send each a copy of the central ideas section and ask them if they'd be willing to spend an hour or two testing the system.
> —Meet with the group and personally act as facilitator to guide them through the assessment steps. Stop when you have tabulated the data from the voting sheets. Ask them if they feel it would be useful to

use the method at an annual retreat.

—Assuming your small group agrees, describe the assessment methodology to your entire senior management group. Show them the results of your pilot test. See if they would be willing to spend a day doing a complete assessment. If they are willing, try it!

◆   ◆   ◆

❑ If you decide to use the method, I would also suggest you use an outside consultant to facilitate the meeting. A consultant normally adds some credibility to the process, can ensure confidentiality during the process, and provide objectivity in assessing the results. However, before hiring consultants for this, have them review the procedure. Be sure you hire someone able and willing to use the method you have selected.

Bottom Lines

➤ Two types of organizational assessment are vital to all organizations:

—Assessment of what the organization is doing: its goals, programs, and policies.

—Assessment of how the organization is doing its work: the health of working processes, like decision-making systems.

➤ Senior managers must allocate organizational time for assessment, and find an appropriate process for performing the assessment. This module focuses on one process that always produces excellent results.

Planning:
Preparing for the Future

Typical Situation

Patrick Donovan, plant manager of a major automobile manufacturer, is unhappy with the status of planning. He's thinking about the changes he'd made to the planning system, and wondering what he did wrong. He thinks, "We used to plan with our regular staff but didn't ever seem to have enough time or expertise to do it right. So I hired a planner. My sense is not much happened. The guy was super smart, but just didn't seem to make an impact. Now he's gone, hired away, left today. Actually I'm kind of glad. Lets us regroup and rethink our planning system. Whatever we do has got to be an improvement. Nothing's happening right now. Must get the staff together. I need some advice on this."

Central Ideas

Planning is the process of matching opportunities with capabilities, recognizing that both are moving targets. Opportunities are continually changing due to factors in the external environment, and organizational capabilities can be

173

changed by importing resources from that external environment. The process of making this match influences and is influenced by the values and mission of the organization. As we plan, we must be open to the possibility of changing anything and everything, including values and mission. Planning must quarrel with success. We must continually ask ourselves: What should we be doing?

How we organize for planning has a big impact on the process. There are two major organizational approaches. One is to have the regular staff periodically put on their "planning hats" and function as the planning team. The other is to organize a separate planning office that does nothing but focus on planning. Both approaches have advantages and disadvantages. Central planning offices ensure that planning is a continuous process; they keep planning on the front burner. Also they can be staffed by people with a special competency in planning. The problem with central planning is that the planners are often ignored or mismanaged by senior managers, leaving them with too little clout and insufficient information to plan effectively.

Having the planning done by the regular staff solves the information problem and brings important realism to the process. But the staff may lack knowledge of planning techniques. Also, unless there is sustained senior-level interest, planning may become sporadic or crisis oriented. It may tend to be done with time left over from operating activities, and it may become bounded by operating concerns and thus lack creativity.

I've seen central planning offices work. But it takes a central planner with superb bureaucratic skills to keep the rest of the organization involved in the planning. Further, the organizational leaders must give the central planner the necessary clout to be effective.

My experience indicates that the best organization for planning is one that uses the regular operating staff for planning, supplemented by a planning-process consultant at times of peak planning activity.

I also have two favorite "musts" about planning. First, you must build an evaluation system into the plan. The system must force periodic evaluation during which you ask if the plan is still feasible, and if it will help the right problem. You must also continue to reevaluate your goals. You want to be sure that you still want to go where the plan is designed to take you.

Second, you must plan with the future (not the existing) environment in mind, honestly facing the facts about the predictability of the external environment. The diagram below indicates that we all need to plan very differently in predictable environments than we do in turbulent or unpredictable environments.

In predictable environments we can use the implementing design. By definition, we know all about the future. We can, therefore, plan long range and comprehensively, with clear goals at the start, seeking a plan that guides our ac-

Planning	
Predictable Environments vs. (Implementing Design)	*Turbulent Environments* (Learning Design)
Long Range	Short Range
Comprehensive	Piecemeal

Plan Guides Decisions and
    Actions
	Decisions and Actions
	    Form the Plan

Clear Goals at the Start	Unclear Goals (Experiment w/goals)
Commit Resources at the Start	Commit Slowly to What Works
Manage by Exception	Assume Things Will Go Wrong
Avoid Conflict	Seek/Use Conflict

Adapted from unpublished class notes of Prof. Robert P. Biller, School of Policy Planning and Development, University of Southern California, with permission.

tions. We can afford to commit major resources early, manage the few things that might go wrong, and avoid conflict (since we know all the answers).

In a turbulent environment we should use a learning design (i.e., act more tentatively, and learn as we go along). Planning should be short range and piecemeal. We must experiment with goals, assume things will go wrong, and commit slowly to what works. Conflict is important because we need all the ideas we can get.

These differences in planning approaches are important to consider. When we think of planning, most of us normally think about the implementing design. But today, more often than not, our environmental conditions have a high degree of uncertainty. If we ignore the environmental turbulence our plans will be off target.

To illustrate, I'll go back many years, to a personal experience in the army. In 1970 I was executive officer (i.e., chief of staff) of a seven-thousand-man separate infantry brigade in Vietnam. In July we were notified that we would be deactivated in mid-October. This meant three months of planning and implementing our inactivation while gradually phasing down our combat operations. To further complicate things, we were one of the first units to inactivate, so we had no tested blueprint of how to proceed.

My brigade commander (a very bright guy) gave some excellent guidance. He said to me: "John, this is going to be tricky. Tell you what—I'll fight the war; you plan the operation to draw us down and get us out on time. And, by the way, let's not generate a mountain of paper work and detailed long-range plans that are out of date before they get in print. Stay with short-range actions so we can learn as we go."

That was great guidance, and that's what we did. We stood

down (i.e., removed from combat) one battalion at a time. Each Saturday we'd have a meeting of the elements being inactivated, and distribute written guidance (for the next week only) in all of the appropriate action areas (e.g., equipment turn-in, turnover of bases to the Vietnamese, personnel release).

Then, during the week, we'd monitor events and make changes to our procedures as necessary. For example, when the authorities refused to accept our trucks for some specific mechanical reason, we knew to fix that problem on trucks the following week. When the Vietnamese demanded that all generators work before accepting base camps, we knew what to do with the next base camp to be turned over.

> ◆ **KEY QUOTE** ◆
>
> **"I don't believe in business plans. If you have a plan, it means you're not prepared for change."**
> **—Brenda French**
> **CEO, French Rags**

As you might expect, we had a lot of high-level visitors inspect our progress. The first thing they'd ask for was our "comprehensive plan." Told of our system of weekly meetings and ever-changing instructions, many visitors were openly skeptical. But we proved them wrong. Things worked fine, because we were smart enough to know that the planning environment was turbulent and required a high degree of planning flexibility—a learning design.

Situation Revisited

Patrick sent the staff a memo telling them of his concerns about planning, and asking them to come to the meeting with ideas to improve the planning system.

They assembled, some with notes. Patrick started things off:

"I don't want to make any decisions today. I just want to get some ideas. Let's go around the table."

Then the ideas came—thick and fast:

"Don't ever hire another central planner. The guy might have known planning, but he didn't know us."

"Right, he had no appreciation for how quickly external conditions change for us."

"He was never going to learn either. The guy never talked to anyone. Worked in isolation."

"Let's go back to our old system. There's no reason we can't do our own planning right in this room. We know our business, and our environment."

Patrick listened a while then spoke up:

"I agree with one thing: no more central planners. But, we had problems doing this with the regular staff. I think we were inhibited by our knowledge of all the implementation difficulties. We didn't want to consider future options that would cause us operational problems. How can we get out of that box?"

Ideas started to flow again. Then Marie Feagan spoke up. She was one of the sharpest at the table, respected by all, quiet till now.

"Patrick, we can do this better as a staff. But I think we need to change our mindset when we come in here to plan. Planning meetings should be different than regular staff meetings. I don't know, maybe even a name change would help. When you call a meeting to plan, call it a "planning group" meeting. We put on a different hat, so to speak. I also think we need some help. A good external consultant who knows planning processes and who can also facilitate our planning meetings: keep us on target, and suggest creative processes that are important to planning, but not necessary at regular staff meetings."

The conversation continued. Support for the idea grew. Patrick knew they'd had a breakthrough. He'd bring this meeting to a close, meet with Marie, flesh out some details and revisit this with the staff next week. Things would get back on track.

Application

❑ Think about your own organization and its planning environment and practices.

—Are you satisfied with the planning system of your organization? Does it produce timely information for decision making?

—Is the future environment of your organization reasonably predictable or highly unpredictable? Does your organization's planning approach match the predictability of the environment?

—When was the last time you examined the effectiveness of your organization's system of planning?

◆ ◆ ◆

❑ Schedule a staff meeting to reflect on the current planning system in the organization.

◆ ◆ ◆

❑ Before meeting on this subject send a copy of the central ideas in this section to each staff member. Ask each to reply anonymously to these questions:

—What do you consider the three major strengths of our planning system?

—What do you consider the three major weaknesses of our planning system?

—What are your three best suggestions to improve our planning system?

❑ Again, before the meeting, send all participants a list of each strength, weakness, and suggestion for improvement that you receive from the staff (omit none). Ask each person to rate each item as follows: strongly agree, agree, neutral, disagree, strongly disagree, or don't know. Array the data on this and use it as the basis for discussion at your meeting.

Bottom Lines

➤ How we organize for planning has a big impact on the process. Planning with existing staff is one approach—staff members periodically put on their planning hats. Appointing a central planner whose sole function is planning is also a possibility. Either approach will work. But certain skills, attitudes, and working relationships are needed to make it work.

—Central planners need clout from the top, technical planning skills, plus strong bureaucratic skills to build internal and external relationships.

—When the staff is used for planning they must develop a creative mindset and not be inhibited unduly by operational difficulties.

➤ Large comprehensive plans are often useful, but they are only appropriate when the environment of the organization is stable and predictable. In turbulent environments it is important to move to more tentative short-range planning, experimenting with both goals and implementation steps.

➤ Evaluation of plans is critical. A specific system for evaluation should be a built-in feature of any plan.

Managing Change:
Making It Easy—Getting It Done

Typical Situation

Dan Taylor, V.P. for human resource management of a manufacturer of snack foods is suddenly uneasy. Several months ago, the management team decided to restructure its assembly line by reclassifying employees from six grade levels to three, expanding their responsibilities, and requiring them to undergo special training and pass qualifying examinations for their new jobs.

It had sounded like a good idea, promising improvements in both productivity and employee morale. But now, just days away from the start of training, Dan's not so sure. A number of good employees have stopped by the HRM office, with real concerns. They don't understand the reason for the changes and are concerned about possible implications for themselves. What will be their new grade? What if they fail the training? Could they lose pay, or their job?

Driving home after talking to six concerned employees today, Dan wonders: "Did we go too fast on this change? Did we fail to build our case and orient people properly? Do we have the right policies and support systems in place? What did we do wrong? What should we do now?"

Central Ideas

Change issues abound in organizations: new bosses, changes in policy and procedures, new equipment, new organizational structures, and new products. Also, change is a permanent, not a transient, phenomena. Therefore, we need a process in place to cope with continual change. We can't just manage change "by exception"—putting bandages on things. To be an effective manager one must also be a good manager of change. And there is a definite technology for doing this.

I am suggesting here a four-step process to plan and manage change. I've used it in dozens of organizations. It works!

1. *Recognize that you are involved in organizational change* (i.e., be conscious that a given problem is a "change" problem). This may seem trivial, but failure to label something as a change can cause us to miss the opportunity to use appropriate change management tools.

2. *Conceptualize a general strategy for dealing with change.* Decide whether you are going to be able to inform and educate people so they will want the change; or whether you will need to use a power strategy, applying a lot of pressure to get the change accomplished. Obviously the educational strategy is best for building commitment to change. But it may not work for everyone. Normally, in designing strategy, we need to consider the use of both educational and power strategies, varying the approach over time and with different constituencies—

◆ **KEY QUOTE** ◆

"There is nothing permanent except change."

—Heraclitus

doing what works, and not feeling guilty about it.

   3. Use the following change principles to design an action plan*:

—Be specific about your goals.

—Be deliberate. Plan the change.

—Get top management support—early!

—Consider timing, and the existing positive and negative trends and forces.

—Demonstrate appropriate respect for the status quo.

—Don't oversell.

—Validate your viewpoint by finding strong evidence,
beyond your own expertise, to support the change.

—Gradually and systematically build support throughout the organization.

—Marshall the necessary external support.

—Welcome resistance to change. Use it to sharpen ideas
and to encourage caution.

—Make the change, once started, easy to stop. Give
powerful skeptics some control over whether to stop
the change.

—Make the cost of change as low as possible. Consider
low-cost pilot testing.

—Make failure costs low for participants.

—Guard against extremists on your planning team. Use
balanced people.

—Anticipate the multiple consequences of change.

—Plan for early and continuous evaluation as part of the
change process, to permit organizational learning.

—Try to institutionalize the change. Make it independent of your personal support.

---

*These points are adapted from unpublished class notes of Professor Robert P.
Biller, School of Policy Planning and Development, University of Southern
California, with permission.

4. *Manage the dynamics of the change process.* Principles can be helpful in the design of specific actions to implement a change strategy. However, it is important to recognize that application of the principles is only the starting point. What is also needed, for successful implementation, is a watchfulness over the dynamics of the process—learning from experience as the change process evolves over time. This step brings closure to the entire change process.

My experience indicates that efforts to systematically design and manage change, using this four-step process, enhance the chances for change ideas to be accepted.

Let me end this section with some lessons I've learned from helping organizations with change over the past twenty years.

- **You Need Top Management Support**

Change may not be possible at all without support from the top. Certainly, change is highly unlikely in the face of skepticism or opposition by the leadership. Thus, change proponents should not invest heavily in a change effort without at least tacit approval by top management. Such support functions as a catalyst for the change. Most importantly, high-level support informs organizational members that there's a high probability of change if they do nothing. Consequently, it helps to crystallize lower-level debate on the change.

- **Develop Balanced Constituencies**

You must be sure to identify all constituencies, and to seek support from each appropriate group. A high degree of support from most constituency groups will not compensate for a failure to win support from a key group.

- **Understand the Importance of Timing**

Timing of the change is of critical importance. It is important to introduce the idea for change when organizational and external conditions will reinforce the change effort. Initiate change, for instance, when business slumps. A second timing issue is the need to gain approval for change and to begin initial activities quickly, in order to capture the parties to agreements. Opportunities often are lost because studies, rightfully designed to build credibility, delay implementation to a point where the departure of key individuals disrupted the change effort.

- **Legitimize the Change Effort**

You cannot be too careful in legitimizing the change effort. Multiple efforts to legitimize should be used whenever possible, and you must never consider the legitimizing effort to be completed. Further, you can never trust that your own personal credibility is sufficient to legitimize the effort. There appears to be some threshold of credibility that must be reached in an organization before change will be accepted as legitimate, and it's hard to know when you've reached that point. So, you must continue efforts to legitimize until you're certain that the idea has been accepted. Supportive views by recognized outside experts or trusted insiders, and favorable evidence from other organizations that have made similar changes, will go a long way toward legitimizing the change.

- **Show Appropriate Concern for the Status Quo**

Change proponents must take a very proactive approach to supporting existing organizational systems and goals while simultaneously pressing for change. A change can be legitimized, and all concerned can consider it valid and useful. However, opposition to the change can still exist simply because organizational members are committed to the status quo. Consequently, you cannot be too careful during planning to give evidence of support for existing organizational goals.

Whenever you push new ideas or programs, there is a natural suspicion that you lack respect for the existing program. You must, from the start, actively seek ways to dispel this feeling.

- **Understand the Advantage of Sharing Risks**

You must extend participation to all appropriate members of the organization, particularly to those with an active role in implementation. One very powerful way to extend participation is to share risks, which gives everyone a stake in the success of the project. Without sharing risks, it is next to impossible to fully share rewards and achieve the level of participation that results in real commitment.

However, you must proceed with some caution here. If you make the risks too high (e.g., loss of job if the project fails), people will be reluctant to participate. So you must seek some tolerable level of risk. For example, you might say to your people: "Look, I won't kid you: Our reputation as a group is a bit on the line here. But I can tell you no one's job is at risk, and the odds of success are so much in our favor that it's worth a little risk."

- **Work to Achieve Organizational Learning**

Proponents of change efforts can have a tendency to overestimate the power of favorable evaluation data in convincing others of the wisdom of the project. Such data are often used as part of the effort to educate people on the wisdom of the change. These educational efforts are worthwhile. They often convince some organization members, generally facilitate persuasion approaches, and may even buffer the heaviness of power strategies. But change proponents should avoid overoptimism or hasty conclusions about the state of learning in the organization. Even though *you* buy the data, others may not.

- **Match Power Usage to the Organizational Context**

Much of the change literature discourages the use of power to achieve change. However, the use of power is often necessary and appropriate in some organizations (e.g., in a hierarchical organization with strong lines of command and authority). The point here is that the use of power is not necessarily bad. It can be acceptable and even necessary, but it should be applied with sensitivity to the organizational context.

● **Monitor the Dynamics of the Change Process**

Key to successful change: monitoring the dynamic nature of the process. Once you take initial actions, you must tend to the task of continuously monitoring progress. Only through this means can you guide the change effort effectively.

● **Avoid a Fixation on Goals and Project Boundaries**

There can be a tendency on the part of change proponents to forget that goals and project boundaries should remain flexible, a part of the dynamic change process. You generally set goals and establish project boundaries early in a project's history and direct your major attention and effort toward achievement of the goals. Research efforts are then often confined to data gathering to determine how well the project is moving toward the established goals. This is not enough. You must also continually examine the suitability of your current goals and make adjustments in goals when appropriate.

In summary, perhaps the most overreaching conclusion about change is the inadequacy of any form of conventional thinking about change. Often we begin a project enamored by the notion of education and with the idea that resorting to power strategies represents failure to some degree. But what is really important is to use the whole range of possible strategies, tailoring strategy to the needs of the organization at the time and to particular constituencies.

> ◆ **KEY QUOTE** ◆
>
> **"If change is to occur, it**
> **must come about through**
> **hard work within the**
> **organization itself."**
> **—Gordon Lippitt**

Another key issue is institutionalization. The whole effort hardly seems worthwhile unless parallel measures are taken toward institutionalization.

The biggest risk to institutionalization is that the change agent might leave the organization before the change fully takes hold. The way to promote institutionalization is to ensure that someone is available to take over who supports the change.

Finally, you must anticipate the unexpected, and in that way try to avoid surprises. Surprises may be inevitable in planned change efforts, but anticipating surprises can both dampen adverse impacts and create new opportunities.

Situation Revisited

Dan decides to call in John Hall, a consultant, for some advice. John has been doing training programs for the firm for three years. He knows the business, the people and, most important, he's written a book on managing change. Dan asks John to spend a day informally talking to people and then meet with him to discuss the situation.

The scene is Dan's office.

"So, John, what's the verdict?"

"People are upset, worried. You already sensed that."

"Can we put things back on track?"

"I think so. Your people like it here. They aren't about to jump ship. But they don't like this sudden change."

"Sudden? We've been talking about this for a year now."

"Not with them. People fear the unknown. And they just don't know enough about this."

"Do we have to postpone the implementation?"

"I'm not sure. But I have a suggestion, a first move."

"I'm all ears."

"Well, I suggest you put out something in writing, this week. It should be addressed personally to each employee. It should acknowledge that you don't feel the change has been handled as well as it should have been. But it should also state your conviction that this is a good change, for the firm and its people. Attribute their concern to your failure to adequately explain things—that's really true. Finally, announce a series of meetings, on company time, at which everyone will be thoroughly briefed and have a chance to ask questions."

"Sounds like a good start—then what?"

"Actually, I'm not finished. Before you hold the briefing, I suggest a small focus group of people you know well to develop the questions you want to answer in the briefing. The obvious questions like: 'Could my pay decrease?' (Hopefully, the answer is no.) 'Can I repeat the training if I fail?' (The answer must be yes.) You won't think of everything, but packaging answers to the most pressing questions will get the meetings off to a good start."

"Then what?"

"Then I'll come back, prowl around for a couple days. Assess the climate. I think then I'll be able to help you move forward. If I think you need to slow things down a bit, I'll let you know."

"Sounds good. Thanks John, as always."

Application

❑ Some of the reactions that individuals have to organizational changes are listed below. Think of some significant change that you have experienced in your career that had an important negative impact on you. Circle the words in the following list that describe how you felt:

depressed	lost	discouraged	rejected
helpless	disappointed	hurt	crushed
drained	vulnerable	used	confused
bored	abused	down	sad
mad	angry	hostile	furious
hate-filled	bitter	irritated	resentful
agitated	envious	disgusted	cheated
happy	delighted	pleased	grateful
agitated	upset	offended	slighted
surprised	relieved	hopeful	enthusiastic
elated	glad	excited	turned on
panicky	frightened	anxious	nervous
embarrassed	ashamed	humiliated	guilty
insecure	ignored	neglected	doubtful
unimportant	regretful	unsure	intimidated
uncertain	left out	unappreciated	competent
confident	determined	proud	fulfilled
capable	needed	secure	important
appreciated	trapped	burdened	overwhelmed
frustrated	torn	driven	exasperated

◆　◆　◆

❑ What could the proponent of the change have done to make the change more acceptable to you personally?

◆　◆　◆

❑ Think of a change effort that your organization completed. Examine the change process using the four-step process suggested here. How could the change have been managed better?

❑ Think of some future change for which you plan to be the proponent. Use the four-step process outlined here to develop an action plan for this change effort.

◆   ◆   ◆

❑ Consider sharing the central ideas of this module with other senior managers in your organization the next time your management group is involved in planning change, to assist the group in its efforts.

◆   ◆   ◆

❑ Consider sharing the central ideas of this module with other senior managers in your organization now, to assist your management group in identifying actions needed regarding ongoing change efforts.

Bottom Lines

➤ Change bothers most people. They fear it and may resist it.

➤ Top-level support for change is essential. Get that first, then gradually build support throughout the organization.

➤ Carefully explain the change, particularly the advantages to each constituency.

➤ Don't oversell the change.

➤ Respect the status quo. It will help win support for the change.

➤ Slowing down a change is normally a good idea.

➤ Keep watching the change during implementation. If something goes wrong, fix it.